"What shall we do—what can we do—with tl
Hebrew Bible of a violent, military, exacting, and ⸺⸺ ⸺ ⸺⸺ cruel one
and only God? How can we cope with this depiction in today's war-torn
world? Juliana Claassens suggests a way. She looks at the Hebrew God
through a feminist lens. She enlists these admittedly rare descriptions as
a female—mourner, mother, and midwife. By so doing, and by
presenting these minority descriptions as metaphors, she decentralizes
violence in favor of life giving, while at the same time avoiding the
difficult issue of tendering God. A book of our times and for our
times."

> —Athalya Brenner, Professor Emeritus of Hebrew Bible,
> University of Amsterdam

"Juliana Claassens writes a compelling and moving book that challenges
the centrality of the violent, punitive God in interpretation and theology.
To broaden our biblical perceptions of God, she zeroes in on biblical
images of God the Deliverer, Mother, Mourner, and Midwife. The result
is a theological refreshment that expands interpretation, addresses pain in
the face of empire, and draws on the women's experience to tell of a life-
giving God. Claassens's book will make an excellent teaching text and
provide resources for interpreters hoping to discover new ways to speak
of the Holy One, ever ancient and ever new."

> —Kathleen M. O'Connor, William Marcellus McPheeters Professor
> of Old Testament Emerita, Columbia Theological Seminary

"Fresh, thought-provoking, and carefully textually based, Claassens
powerfully demonstrates contemporary ethical implications of Old
Testament female metaphors for God as Deliverer. Showing how these
female metaphors 'interrupt' the dominant Liberator-Warrior imagery,
Claassens places them in fruitful conversation with trauma theory, postcolonial thought, and literature from a variety of cultural contexts.
Academically significant and accessibly written for seminary and church
study audiences."

> —Katharine Doob Sakenfeld, William Albright Eisenberger
> Professor of Old Testament Literature and Exegesis,
> Princeton Theological Seminary

"The Bible often ties together images of God as Liberator with troublesome images of God as violent Warrior (Exod. 15:3; Isa. 42:13). Julie Claassens argues that there are more helpful, alternative metaphors for God's liberating work in the Hebrew Bible that have been neglected and need to be recovered: God as Mourner (Jer. 8-9), as Nurturing Mother (Isa. 42; 49), and as Life-Giving Midwife (Ps. 22; 71). Claassens offers a bold and creative work of biblical theology born out of her South African context that offers good news for those marginalized and traumatized by oppressive empires today."

—Dennis Olson, Charles T. Haley Professor of Old Testament Theology, Princeton Theological Seminary

"Drawing from recent work in trauma and Holocaust studies, exile, and postcolonial interpretation, Claassens invites us to reconsider the oppressive link between God and violent warrior imagery. By bringing together three relational metaphors for God that have often been muted—Mourner, Mother, and Midwife—Claassens convincingly redeems God as a Deliverer to promote healing and hope in our troubled time. Claassens urges us to speak of God's power in a different way to transform education and worship and cultivate compassion and critical thinking. Her prophetic vision makes this a must-read for church leaders and seminarians everywhere."

—Denise Dombkowski Hopkins, Professor of Old Testament, Wesley Theological Seminary

Mourner, Mother, Midwife

Mourner, Mother, Midwife

*Reimagining God's Delivering Presence
in the Old Testament*

L. Juliana M. Claassens

WESTMINSTER
JOHN KNOX PRESS
LOUISVILLE · KENTUCKY

First edition
Published by Westminster John Knox Press
Louisville, Kentucky

12 13 14 15 16 17 18 19 20 21—10 9 8 7 6 5 4 3 2 1

Book design by Sharon Adams
Cover design by Dilu Nicholas
Cover illustration: Moses in the Bullrushes *1983.95.197* © *Henry Ossawa Tanner/Smithsonian American Art Museum, Gift of Mr. and Mrs. Norman Robbins*

Library of Congress Cataloging-in-Publication Data

Claassens, L. Juliana M.
    Mourner, mother, midwife: reimagining God's delivering presence in the Old Testament / L Juliana M Claassens. — 1st ed.
        p. cm.
    Includes bibliographical references.
    ISBN 978-0-664-23836-0 (alk. paper)
    1. Femininity of God. I. Title.
    BT153.M6C417 2013
    231—dc23   2012016842

Most Westminster John Knox Press books are available at special quantity discounts when purchased in bulk by corporations, organizations, and special-interest groups. For more information, please e-mail SpecialSales@wjkbooks.com.

For Julia, Annette, Vigné, and Kathy
(my Grandmother, Mother, Mother-in-Law, and
"Doktormutter") as well as for every mother who,
with limited resources and in very difficult
circumstances, embodied something of God's
delivering presence

Contents

Acknowledgments

The birthing story of a book is often, as in the case of real life, long, complicated, and exceedingly painful. But as my mother used to say: when you hold the baby in your arms, the suffering rapidly recedes into the background.

Mourner, Mother, Midwife is no exception. From its initial gestation as a kernel of an idea for my Doktormutter (doctoral supervisor), Kathy Sakenfeld's festschrift, it slowly grew over the next five years into a fully developed entity in its own right that miraculously survived one of the worst economic downturns in U.S. history.

The gestation period happened during the time I spent teaching at Baptist Theological Seminary in Richmond, Virginia, and Wesley Theological Seminary in Washington, DC, before returning after thirteen years in the United States to teach at my alma mater, Stellenbosch University, in one of the most beautiful student towns in the world, Stellenbosch, South Africa.

There were a number of midwives along the way. My appreciation to Jon Berquist, Neil Elliott, and in particular Marianne Blickenstaff, who managed to finally deliver this baby despite the financial constraints facing publishers these days. I am deeply thankful for her careful editing, her vision, and her determination that made it possible for this book to see the light of day.

Also a word of thanks to the numerous birthing coaches—the faithful companions who read and commented on this book: Katharine Doob Sakenfeld, Dennis Olson, Bruce Birch, Julia O'Brien, Kathleen O'Connor, Bridgette Green; my colleagues at the various institutions I called home during the time of writing this book, including the Bible department of BTSR (Mark Biddle, Sandra Hack Polaski, Richard Vinson, Scott Spencer) as well as my current department of Old and New Testament at Stellenbosch University, who have so warmly welcomed and made space for me (Hendrik Bosman, Louis Jonker, Jeremy Punt, Elna Mouton). My conversation partners from other theological disciplines (Robert Vosloo, Beth Newman, Beverly Mitchell, Tom Reynolds, Rachel Baard, Johan Cilliers) have all cultivated my interdisciplinary interest, which found its way into this book. Thank you also to my assistant Annemarie de Kock, who did a lot of tedious work on the way to the final project, as well as Len Hansen for his careful copyediting.

And then there are my family and friends on both sides of the Atlantic Ocean who have been so supportive over the past years regarding my vocation and my migrating existence. In particular I want to mention my two wonderful stepchildren, Jana and Roux, for the many rich experiences we have shared and for the intense conversations regarding every topic under the sun. And Robert, my best friend and conversation partner and now also my colleague at Stellenbosch University: It is difficult to find words to capture your contribution in my life. Thank you for reminding me of Jacques Derrida's notion of the "possible as impossible" as it found expression in Richard Kearney's *The God Who May Be*:

> If what happens is only that which is possible in the sense of that which is anticipated and expected, then it is not an event in the true sense. For an event is only possible in so far as it comes from the impossible. An event can only happen, in other words, when and where the "perhaps" lifts all presumptions and assurances about what might be and lets the future come as future, that is, the arrival of the impossible. The "perhaps" thus solicits a "yes" to what is still to come, beyond all plans, programs and predictions. (94)

Chapter 1

Liberating God-Language?

The metaphor of God as Liberator is one of the most compelling metaphors in the Bible: the account of how God delivered Israel from a life of slavery and oppression in Egypt serves people in situations of oppression everywhere as inspiration to fight for justice and liberty for all. Beyond the ethnic particularity of the original story, the biblical narrative of deliverance is paradigmatically understood to refer to the liberation of people who find themselves trapped in the chains of oppression all over the world. Thus, the Moses who was cited in the African American spiritual to "go down, Moses, way down in Egypt's land" and who was to "tell ol' Pharaoh, 'Let my people go'" is embodied in a Martin Luther King Jr. in the United States, in a Desmond Tutu in South Africa, and in every leader who stands up for justice and righteousness in the name of the Deliverer God.

However, it is quite difficult to separate the joyous celebration of victory and liberation on behalf of the suffering and oppressed from the violent warrior imagery that is regularly used in biblical traditions in

1

conjunction with the image of God as Liberator. Students taking my "Introduction to the Hebrew Bible" courses often reveal their confusion and even disgust when it comes to the image of the mighty Liberator-Warrior God who, with a strong hand and a mighty arm, smites Israel's enemies—for example, the image of God using wind and sea as weapons to bring the Egyptian army to its knees; the infamous *ḥerem* texts, according to which God commanded the complete annihilation of the people of the land of Canaan (Deut. 20:16–17; Josh. 6); the apocalyptic image in Isaiah 63 of God treading the winepress, his robes stained by the blood of Israel's enemies. The image of God with blood on his hands is troubling indeed.

THE LIBERATOR-WARRIOR GOD-FOR-US?

My own need to deal with these difficult texts is rooted in two concerns that have profoundly shaped my vocation as teacher and writer: First, my experience growing up in apartheid South Africa sensitized me to the dangers of claiming the Liberator-Warrior God for political gain. In his book *God for Us?* which analyzes numerous sermons that were preached in the Dutch Reformed Church from 1960 to 1980, Johan Cilliers shows how, for Afrikaner people, "the national history is surrounded with a radiance of holiness and becomes salvific history."[1] Cilliers quotes from a sermon that shows a particularly graphic example of the metaphor of God as Liberator-Warrior,

> Farmers moved into a cruel and wild country where predators and barbarians were a dangerous threat, but in lonely farmhouses, the Word of the Lord saved a nation from being frightened away.[2]

Invoking Psalm 62:6, this sermon draws on the memory of God's faithfulness and liberating actions in Afrikaner history, which should encourage the white minority to trust in God, who will save them (by violent means, if necessary) from the perceived threat from the black majority.[3]

During my years teaching at a number of U.S. institutions, it was important for me to help my students realize that the South African experience reflected in the sermon cited above is a way to face their own, often painful, American history, which has also been told in terms of deliverance and redemption. As was the case in my native South Africa, this "liberation" all too often occurred to the detriment of others. From the perspective of the marginalized members of society the American grand narrative of redemption looks very different. Flora Keshgegian writes, "In that grand narrative they are damned, demonized and brutalized. They are robbed of and displaced from their lands, denied their freedom, labeled as primitive and savaged, and forced into giving up cultural and religious practices—all in the name of civilization and salvation."[4]

The image of God as Liberator-Warrior is still evoked to advance the social and political agendas of the powers that be. In recent years, particularly in the wake of the war in Iraq, an increasing number of theologians have raised critical questions regarding the way theological formulations such as the image of God as Liberator-Warrior continue to be employed by those in power. Scholars such as Catherine Keller and Elisabeth Schüssler Fiorenza have turned their attention to the way empire thinking has seeped into theological language and practice, and vice versa. Catherine Keller consequently argues that "Christian theology suffers from an imperial condition." According to Keller, "Christianity spoke in the many tongues of empire—nations and languages colonized by Rome, before that Greece, before that Babylon which had first dispersed the Jews in imperial space."[5] The result of this preoccupation with empire is that a theology of omnipotence has profoundly shaped a policy of American imperialism.[6] These scholars, by critically engaging with the way in which power and empire function in theopolitical discourse, seek to rethink or "recode" the very concept of power and to provide modes of alternative thinking.[7]

My work has also been dedicated to a critical as well as constructive engagement with biblical metaphors for God that have the potential to be misused or abused by those in power. A metaphor such as God as Liberator-Warrior, which assumes an inherent connection between God and violence, challenges students to take the text seriously—to ask questions such as, Why did Israel choose to portray the Liberator God in such violent terms? It is helpful, for instance, to understand that the rhetoric of violence that permeates biblical traditions comes from a time in which Israel was overrun by superpowers. The discourse on divine force is thus best understood as Israel's response to the violent trauma experienced at the hands of its oppressors. Insight into the literary and socio-cultural context from which these texts and images arose is of paramount importance in order to make some kind of sense of this often-troubling language for God.

Moreover, contemporary examples of how the image of God as Liberator-Warrior has been used in a variety of contexts to the detriment of others serve as poignant reminders that the language and metaphors we use for God greatly affect the world we live in. Given the complex geopolitical situation in which we find ourselves, this innate power of God-language to guide and to shape people's beliefs and actions challenges us to consider some alternative, more responsible ways of speaking of the Deliverer God.

WOMAN WARRIOR
AND THE LIBERATOR-WARRIOR GOD

A second concern that informs my commitment to critically consider the language people use when referring to God flows from my position as a feminist biblical theologian who seeks to deconstruct harmful interpretations of the biblical text (particularly pertaining to gender) as well as to reconstruct theological readings that promote justice and equality for all. The fact that, for the greater part of the history of the Christian tradition, the metaphor of God as mighty Liberator-Warrior has been understood in terms of hierarchical structures of power, grounded in values such as domination, control, and triumph, has proven a key point of concern to feminist scholars such as Rita Nakashima Brock, whose critique of authoritarian, hierarchical representations of God I shall introduce in one of the chapters of this book.[8]

A fruitful avenue for exploring gender, power, and violence is the fascinating image of the Woman Warrior as it occurs in the interrelated stories of Deborah and Jael, told in Judges 4–5. In a situation of extreme duress these two women emerged as liberators of their people, both of them by resorting to violence in order to save the Israelites. Susan Ackerman explores how these two women, who served as the means by which God liberated God's people, each emerged in her own way as the embodiment of the Divine Warrior himself. Deborah, who is said to have mustered the troops and sent them forth in battle, is portrayed as the deliverer of her people and can rightly be described as God's human representative who will execute the holy war on earth.[9] The "female assassin," Jael, brought to an end the battle that Deborah had initiated when she used a tent peg to annihilate the enemy leader, Sisera.

When considering the notion of the Woman Warrior in the biblical traditions, I often begin my classes by showing a short music video that contains scenes from the television series *Xena, Warrior Princess*. The images of the hypersexualized, skimpily clad Xena outfighting every male warrior who comes her way offers an interesting way to start the conversation, as it helps to identify students' preconceptions about gender stereotypes. To see a female warrior who breaks all the traditional stereotypes of women as demure, soft-spoken, and weak challenges many students' understanding of the way they and/or their communities think about the nature of women in comparison to the nature of men. The conversation in class then naturally moves on to questions of whether gender is biologically determined or socially constructed—to cite Simone de Beauvoir's famous dictum, "One is not born, but becomes a woman" (suggesting the latter position).[10] Moreover, the portrayal of the female warrior in the stories of Deborah and Jael further demonstrates that particular gender roles and assumptions about gender roles are never static, but rather change over time. Therefore, gender constructions cannot be assumed to be universally true; rather, they reflect the reigning values in particular cultural and temporal locations.

Class discussions often will turn to the question of whether the image of the woman warrior can be considered a helpful image for women today. As a rule, students tend to be divided on this issue—some usually see the image of the woman warrior as a strong figure that symbolizes the empowerment of women (a woman in one of my classes once actually told her fellow students how she threw her daughter a Xena-themed birthday party!). Similarly, several feminist scholars have argued that stories depicting the woman warrior constitute an image of empowerment, of women fighting back against male domination and oppression. Susan Niditch, for instance, regards Jael as a symbol of "directed action, self-assertion, and consciousness on the part of the underdog." For Niditch, Jael is an instance of the victim fighting back, penetrating the penetrator in ironic fashion with the phallic symbol of a tent peg.[11] And in her postcolonial reading of the postbiblical book Judith, Musa Dube considers the female assassin, which forms the main character of the book, a heroine who resists colonializing forces.[12]

On the other hand, some students usually agree strongly with feminist interpreters who are troubled by the violence associated with the image of the woman warrior. They ask whether this portrayal of women resorting to violence does not merely perpetuate the male hierarchical model evident in the Liberator-Warrior metaphor outlined above.[13] Given my concerns about the dangerous potential of God-language to serve as the catalyst and legitimization of war, the violence inherent in the figure of the female warrior constitutes, to my mind, a serious impediment. A YouTube clip[14] of a determined former British Prime Minister, Margaret Thatcher, staunchly defending her decision to invade the Falkland Islands brings across this point particularly well—the Prime Minister's unflinching, icy-cold resolve raises all kinds of questions regarding females in positions of leadership, in violence and in war.

Once again, it is important to understand the image of the woman warrior in its socio-historical context. For Susan Ackerman, the stories of female warriors such as Deborah, Jael, Judith, and the unnamed woman of Thebez (Judg. 9) who resisted established patterns of gendered behavior normative in their culture, which resulted in their emergence as leaders in Israel's military feats, make most sense in the context of stories about Anath, the ancient Near Eastern warrior goddess.[15] Furthermore, Deborah Sawyer maintains that gender reversal is used as a strategy to denote the failure of human (male) leadership, which forms a central theme in the Deuteronomistic tradition and the book of Judges per se. Sawyer arguers, "In the topsy-turvy world of Judges, controlled and yet not controlled by God, gendered behavior patterns are once more turned on their head and a mighty warrior is ignominiously slain by a woman."[16] Beyond the effect of using women as agents of male shame, we could also consider the notion that the image of the warrior woman may be an expression of a beleaguered people's hope and desire that God—even by the hand of a most unlikely leader—will bring salvation to those in the most desperate of circumstances.

To understand why the biblical writers portrayed God and God's human representatives in such violent ways is, once again, only a first step in the hermeneutical process. As in the previous section, which considered the dangers inherent in the misuse (abuse) of the divine metaphor of God as Liberator-Warrior, it is vital to ask the ethical type of questions, too— such as the one introduced in the previous section: Is the violent language underlying the image of the divine Liberator-Warrior, male or female, the best language for our time? The fact that a female warrior can embody the divine Liberator-Warrior does not solve the problems raised earlier regarding divine violence and the effect of God-language on those followers who emulate a violent God. And in terms of feminist theologians' goal to work not only toward gender but also toward racial equality, it remains debatable whether the link between gender and violence contributes to a world built on justice and equality for all.

Precisely because I deem the metaphor of God as Liberator to be such an important expression of God's relationship with a fragile world (on a personal, communal, and global level I am convinced that we need a Deliverer God now more than ever), I hope to offer in this book some alternative means of speaking about God's deliverance that resist the violence and bloodshed associated with this particular metaphor. It is by creatively engaging with tradition in light of the minor or muted voices in the text that we are able to speak in new contexts, with their particular challenges. This dynamic understanding of introducing alternative metaphors to talk about God's deliverance may indeed offer new perspectives on the traditional metaphor, which will allow it to thrive in new and exciting ways.

REIMAGINING GOD AS DELIVERER

The central argument of this book is that, amid the rhetoric of violence that often marks the biblical discourse, there are also other metaphors that speak of God's deliverance—metaphors that can be used to expand the meaning of the all-important metaphor of God as Liberator. In this regard, I shall use the metaphor of God as Deliverer to denote God's deliverance as opposed to the violent portrayal of the traditional Liberator-Warrior metaphor for God. In the following chapters, I shall turn to three metaphors for God that are used in conjunction with God's acts of deliverance in biblical traditions: God as Mourner or Wailing Woman (Jer. 8:22–9:1), God as Mother (Isa. 42:14; 49:13–15), and God as Midwife (Ps. 22:9–10; 71:6). It is significant that two of these images are associated with childbirth, which presents us with the opportunity to use connotations of "delivery" in the context of childbirth for portraying God as the Deliverer God. These metaphors offer rich possibilities of an alternative image of God that is rooted not in death and destruction, but in engaged, life-enhancing acts as well as a deep-seated compassion for the suffering, the vulnerable, and the powerless.

The metaphors of Mourner, Mother, and Midwife may not be the first images to come to mind when we think about God as Deliverer. For one, in terms of mere narrative (poetic) space—that is, the number of texts in which these metaphors occur—these three metaphors cannot be considered to be prominent in the biblical discourse. However, we live in a time of superpowers that seek to devour those who are in their way; a time of a growing sense of the frailty and vulnerability of the human condition due to the trauma inflicted by 9/11; a time that saw war in Iraq and Afghanistan, and an ongoing global recession. In such a time, the metaphors of God as Mourner, Mother, and Midwife who responded to the trauma Israel experienced during the Babylonian exile and its aftermath may be exactly what we need in order to think differently about God's acts of deliverance. These metaphors are representative of Israel's journey in a particular, significant, and traumatic time in its history. It shows how Israel journeyed from tears to new life. Individually as well as collectively, these unconventional ways of speaking about God's deliverance of a beleaguered people may offer fresh and creative insights into our own understanding of what it means when we call God a Deliverer God.

I chose the metaphors of God as Mourner, Mother, and Midwife for the following reasons: First, all three occur in key biblical texts that in some way relate to the Babylonian exile. This tumultuous period in Israel's history had a profound impact on its sense of self as well as on its perception of God, particularly on its belief in the Deliverer God. Believers who inadvertently saw their lives and their beliefs challenged, if not destroyed, were forced to reconsider the way they understood God's deliverance in terms of their tragic reality—particularly in those instances where liberation seemed to be nowhere on the horizon.

The metaphors of God as Mourner, Mother, and Midwife, which all relate to people's attempts at dealing with trauma and its lingering effects, may offer the potential to speak to people who are dealing with deep-seated experiences of pain today.[17] For people trying to survive in a chaotic world where they increasingly have to accept that guarantees do not exist and that things change without warning, these nontraditional metaphors for God as Deliverer may stretch the imagination to consider from a fresh perspective our own complex situations as well as how God relates to the ambiguities of this world.

It is significant that there was no quick resolution to the trauma caused by the Babylonian exile. We find evidence in the biblical text that, after this initial calamity, further traumatic experiences followed: maltreatment by subsequent empires; painful infighting between the returning exiles and the locals who never left; the destruction of the Second Temple in 70 CE; the Diaspora; the persecution of Jews and Christians throughout the ages. These traumatic experiences extending across generations suggest that there are indeed no simple solutions to the situations of conflict of our own day. The task of doing theology is, therefore, a continuing process of seeking to include into our conversations the ways we talk about God in light of the realities of life that are sometimes far more messy and tragic than we would like them to be.

Moreover, in the biblical texts that respond to the exile and its aftermath we see evidence of believers who had to cope not only with physical destruction and loss but also with seeing their deeply rooted beliefs torn down or ruptured.[18] Without negating the extent of their pain or justifying their suffering, the creative metaphors for God such as a Mourner, Mother, and Midwife reveal glimpses of a new understanding of God that emerged from Israel's profoundly traumatic experience of the exile and its aftermath.

Second, the metaphors of God as Mourner, Mother, and Midwife constitute counter voices in the biblical text that offer a rich resource for considering how to do (or not to do) theology amid the empire(s). A key characteristic of much of the biblical corpus is that it originated in the shadow of the empire, constituting a mix between theology in service of those in power and theology that resists those in power. For this reason we find, in numerous biblical texts, rhetoric that was to a large extent shaped by the looming shadow of the mighty empires that in steady succession oppressed Israel. And yet, if we look closely—sometimes just below the surface—we find texts and fragments of texts that represent a counter or subversive rhetoric, something that James C. Scott has termed "hidden transcripts."[19]

The metaphors of God as Mourner, Mother, and Midwife can thus be considered as subversive voices that offer an important alternative to empire theology. These voices that interrupt the major story line of God as mighty Liberator-Warrior allow us to develop a different understanding of God as Deliverer, which may inform our own way of being in the world: one that is based on values such as mercy, commitment to life, and concern for the other and that directly opposes the empire's drive to show no mercy, to humiliate, and to destroy. In the case of the metaphor of God as a Wailing Woman in particular, we see how the emphasis on God's tears in Jeremiah 8:22–9:1 offers a poignant alternative understanding of the God who just might act as Israel's Deliverer once again.

Third, it is noteworthy that all three these metaphors (Mourner or Wailing Woman, Mother, and Midwife) are female in nature, employing connotations that are associated with female experiences. Continuing the theme of counter voices that necessitate a reading beyond the surface of the text, I suggest that these female voices have the potential to help infuse the metaphor of God as Deliverer with new significance.

Beyond the inherent shock value of the use of female metaphors for God alongside more traditional male metaphors, which may help people grasp the important insight that God is neither male nor female, but that both female and male metaphors are used to image God, there is another benefit in focusing on these female voices in the biblical text: Feminist theologians have been particularly good at noticing these minor or muted voices in the text—voices that, according to Jacqueline Lapsley, are often "extremely subtle" and "murmuring beneath the surface."[20] Attention to these muted voices in the text can indeed render some exciting interpretative and theological possibilities. Gina Hens-Piazza, for example, focuses on the story of the two starving women who came before the king after they had been reduced to eating one of the women's children (2 Kgs. 6:24–33). Throughout her interpretation, Hens-Piazza shows how important it is not only to focus on the stories of the kings but also to really see the plight of these two unnamed women. She argues that the mothers were "dwarfed and rendered insignificant" by the "national and international power struggles," much like the thousands of nameless victims we see—or rather, do not see—in newspapers and on television screens and the Internet.[21]

Hens-Piazza's imaginative interpretation that gives voice to the plight of these seemingly insignificant characters is a prime example of how, by taking note of the muted voices in the text, the reader is helped to become more attentive to the voices in society that are muted or disregarded on a daily basis. Attention to these two women thus challenges us "to confront what is lost when only the so-called 'major' characters are studied or when only the people deemed important by cultural standards are considered." As Hens-Piazza rightly notes, "As the fullness of meaning in a biblical tale increases when each and every character is assessed, so too is the fullness of life itself extended when each person is regarded as worthy of attention."[22]

In this regard, it is significant that the three metaphors for God featured in this book are intrinsically relational in nature, drawing our attention to the other. Thus the wailing woman weeps over a person(s); the mother gives birth to a child whom she will nurture and rear until the child can stand on its own feet; the midwife assists the mother in bringing the baby into the world. As I shall show in the chapters that follow, these metaphors draw our attention to images of God as caring for and supporting those who are vulnerable, those in pain, and those reeling under the effects of unjust power structures. These metaphors serve as vivid reminders that it is possible to transform a discourse of violence, hatred, and destruction into a discourse of hope, life, and love.

I shall try to demonstrate, in particular, how these female metaphors that are found in selected biblical texts encourage us to ask critical questions regarding God's power and the impact of uncritical appropriations of this power for human power structures. The very presence of female metaphors in the biblical text plays a significant role in deconstructing the prevalent hierarchical understanding of a male God as Liberator-Warrior that has dominated much of Hebrew Bible scholarship. In particular, these female metaphors for God offer us the opportunity to continue talking about God's power, albeit in a different way.

Finally, we should realize that using female metaphors for God that are rooted in values such as love, relationality, mutuality, and compassion—values that have been typically associated with women, who have for the most part served as the caregivers in society—offers a critique of essentialism; that is, of the tendency to employ narrow gender stereotypes that maintain that all women *are* a certain way or, even worse, that all women *should be* a certain way. I would be the first person to argue for the necessity to move beyond narrow gender stereotypes and essentialist arguments of the nature of women and values that have been used in the past, and unfortunately still are used, to place constraints on women who have made progress in breaking the mold and cracking the glass ceiling. In this regard, Catherine Keller's expression "let she who is without essences cast the first stone!" reminds us: whenever we begin to speak, we speak in categories, abstractions, and generalizations—a practice that makes speech possible.[23] Moreover, we are also faced with the reality that, in terms of the culture in which the biblical texts arose, certain gender stereotypes and values *did* apply and were employed by biblical writers in their theological reasoning. As I shall show in this book, these stereotypes and values, furthermore, actually function as a counter voice to the dominant discourse of domination and the empire's unbridled use of force.

What is necessary is not to utterly avoid speaking about God in terms of gender categories, for this would cut us off from the wealth of female experience that could broaden and enrich our theological conversation. I rather suggest that we employ female experiences in a descriptive sense, coupled with the added commitment to problematize gender stereotypes and to show instances where they break down or are rendered immaterial. For instance, moving beyond a narrow gender dichotomy, an underlying assumption of this book is that *both* men and women would be well served to grow in the values that in the biblical text have been typically associated with women; the reason being that the world actually would be a much better (and safer) place if these values could become an integral part of the way all of us relate to one another.

RECOGNIZING COMPLEXITY

The alternative understanding of God as Deliverer developed in this book and inspired by the metaphors of God as Mourner, Mother, and Midwife will seek to attend to the complexity in the text that mirrors the complexity in the world. In the first instance, we should note that the biblical witness offers no single solution to the challenges Israel had to face regarding the trauma of the exile. The diversity of literature that grew out of the aftermath of the exile illustrates the variety of responses to the tragedy and its lingering effects.[24]

Not all of these responses are equally advantageous. Some of the theological suppositions reflected in these biblical texts constitute a coping strategy that sought to make sense of the nightmare Israel was experiencing. In this regard, Daniel Smith-Christopher (for example) argues that, in order to make sense of the world and to restore identity, a narrative that has been handed down to the victim is taken and reconfigured with new significance.[25] As will be seen, particularly in chapter 3, the image of God's sovereignty and power—which underlies the foundational metaphor of God as Liberator-Warrior (indeed an important image in the biblical mind-set)—gains new significance in the exiles' attempts to deal with the crisis brought about by the Babylonian forces. Prophets like Jeremiah and Deutero-Isaiah applied the traditional Deuteronomistic theology of retribution to the catastrophe of the exile, depicting the Babylonian Empire as the instrument of the sovereign God, and the destruction of Jerusalem and the mass deportation of its inhabitants as part of God's plan to teach God's wayward child, Israel, a lesson.[26]

Even though this is indeed the view presented by many of the prophets and the historical books, Marvin Sweeney reminds us that, in the wake of the Shoah, the uncritical acceptance of a charge that the victims of evil are responsible for their own suffering is unconscionable. Sweeney shows that there is no agreement in the Hebrew Bible on this particular view of theodicy. Books such as Job, Lamentations, and Esther offer dissenting voices and raise questions that challenge the reader to reflect critically on this foundational issue.[27]

Yet, quite often in biblical interpretation, the uncritical, almost literalistic application of the prophetic explanation that God uses superpowers such as Babylon and Assyria to punish Israel (e.g., Isa. 5:26–30; 10:5–6) is offered as explanation for the tragedy of the exile. This view is particularly disconcerting if we take into account how a direct application of these views without much critical reflection would be regarded in contemporary situations of pain and suffering. In such a scenario, we could argue that God used the hijackers who crashed into the World Trade Center and the Pentagon to punish the United States for turning away from God. Or, consider the unfortunate remarks by someone like Jerry Falwell (corroborated by Pat Robertson) that placed the blame for the 9/11 attacks on "the feminists, 'abortionists,' homosexuals and defenders of civil liberties."[28]

The former coping strategy may not only be unhelpful, it may indeed be harmful to contemporary believers. Smith-Christopher argues that such "theologies of 'God's punishment' . . . could lead to a destructive self-image and sense of hopelessness in renewing or reviving people's religious and social identity or existence."[29] Moreover, neither a "blaming the victim" strategy nor scapegoating, which plays off people's prejudices and fears, is beneficial in dealing with extreme tragedy.

In our encounter with the abovementioned biblical texts, and particularly in the application of these texts in our theological constructions, it is of the utmost importance to engage in a process of critical though sympathetic interpretation. It may be that we do not always agree with the theological answers that the biblical writers gave in their coming to grips with suffering and loss. While we can understand that their theological response formed part of the process of dealing with the shattering of their world, such an "answer" may not be the best interpretative option to pursue today. Nevertheless, the process of doing theology in the midst of the messiness and complexities that surround us is something that we should continue in our ongoing attempts to make sense of the world. What is more, the fact that the biblical text does not provide neatly packaged answers helps us to understand the necessity of maintaining the tension within the ambiguities and complexities of our own theological reflection.

It is only natural that people desire closure. One of my students recently bemoaned the fact that, although she now understands more of the complexity evident in the biblical traditions, she still wishes that things were less complicated: simple and straightforward. Of course the reality of life—the very nature of human existence—is that it is messy, complex, ambiguous, tragic, joyful, and beautiful; often all at once. No wonder literature—and in the case of the Bible, religious literature—regularly follows suit.

Second, when we use biblical texts to reimagine the Deliverer God it is important to heed Edward Said's warning that one natural consequence of trauma is nationalism. In a number of biblical texts we find among the exiles, in their attempts to survive, what Said calls "an exaggerated sense of group solidarity, passionate hostility to outsiders, even those who may in fact be in the same predicament as you." It is indeed most tragic, as Said observes, to be "exiled by exiles," that is, to experience being uprooted by people who have been exiles themselves.[30]

In engaging with the biblical text, we thus have to be aware that, besides all the inspirational accounts of God's acts of deliverance on behalf of God's people in bondage, it also contains numerous examples of what Smith-Christopher calls counter stories gone bad. A primary example would be Ezra's opposition to mixed marriages and his treatment of foreign wives (Ezra 9:10–10:5; see also Neh. 13:23–27). The narratives that are intended to help people deal with trauma and reconstruct their fragmented lives may in fact be highly detrimental, as they base their reconstructive efforts on scapegoating yet another group.[31]

This response to trauma serves as a warning to us all when considering the impact of God's deliverance in our contemporary context(s). As mentioned above, the complexities within the biblical text require of us to read critically, though with sensitivity. Therefore, it is important to understand, on the one hand, why these interpretations were put forth by biblical writers who had experienced unthinkable pain and suffering at the hand of enemy empires. On the other hand, in order to avoid perpetuating the same suffering in the lives of others, we would do well to resist the dominant reading and rather follow the counter voices in the biblical witness—voices that may not be easy to hear, particularly if they speak of justice, healing, or compassion.

Third, when considering an alternative understanding of God as Deliverer, we have to take into account that the biblical text's version of the exile is told from the perspective of the former elite who had occupied positions of power and privilege before they were taken away into captivity. It is this group's experience of trauma and the different theological responses of the trauma survivors that are reflected in much of the biblical text. Thus, when reading these texts that talk about the exile and its impact on people, we have to be mindful of the fact that their story is not the whole story.

In this regard, scholars like Robert Carroll have identified the "myth of the empty land"; that is, the view presented in the biblical text that depicts the exile of "all" of Israel and their subsequent return to an inherently empty land.[32] The classic statement by the postcolonial scholar Gayatri Chakravorty Spivak seems to apply well to this situation: "The subaltern . . . cannot speak." Spivak raises awareness of the very existence of the "subaltern" peoples in the biblical text who are deemed to be inferior to and "other" (Latin: *alter*) than those who hold the power; that is, those who are poor, marginalized, excluded, oppressed, or exploited. Their voices are perhaps heard most clearly in the book of Lamentations.[33]

As noted before, a key assumption of this book relates to the importance of taking note of the minor voices in the text, those voices that are found below the surface of the dominant narrative. In this regard, it is worth noting that feminist theologians have long since struggled with the question of how to glean a hopeful message from literature written exclusively by men for men. If we were to dismiss all biblical texts written from positions of power, not much would be left. These biblical texts still represent an important theological witness, containing examples of how people of centuries ago experienced God in the darkest times of their lives. With a little extra effort, we can join feminist, womanist, and mujerista theologians, as well as women of the Two-Thirds World who have become quite adept at noticing the voices in the shadows, imagining the plight of those men and women who are struggling to let their voices be heard.

By focusing intentionally on the minor voices in the text, we may get into the practice of telling our own story differently so as to include the voices and the concerns of the other. Attention to the muted voices in the text may, in particular, help to foster language for God that can help us to be in touch with the pain and scars that mark the reality of our own lives as well as the lives of many of our neighbors, near and far.

JOURNEYING FROM TEARS TO NEW LIFE

As noted before, the metaphors of God as Mourner, Mother, and Midwife are not the only counter voices in the biblical text. However, these three voices that encourage us to rethink the metaphor of God as Deliverer are representative of Israel's continuing journey between death and life, despair and hope. This book will demonstrate how these three metaphors for God offer resources to contemporary readers to face the challenges of an increasingly complex and violent world: to embrace pain bravely, to be open to new possibilities even while facing the brokenness of the present reality, and to engage in action on behalf of those who are most vulnerable and in need. This book will proceed along the following lines:

Chapter 2 introduces the metaphor of God as Mourner or Wailing Woman. We shall encounter a number of texts from the book of Jeremiah, situated mainly during the extreme suffering of the Babylonian exile. These texts are filled with tears. The tears of the wailing women in Jeremiah 9:17–20 [MT 16-19] join the fountain of tears cried by the prophet and by God in Jeremiah 8:21–9:1 [MT 8:21–23], as well as the tears of Rachel, who is weeping inconsolably in Jeremiah 31:15. I shall show how the metaphor of a Wailing Woman or a Mourner offers a particularly fitting description of the mood of this period, seeing that the only appropriate response to the scenes of death and destruction is lamentation. However, despite the raw descriptions of suffering and pain, among these texts from Jeremiah we also find the first flickering of hope in the midst of despair as the role is explored of the wailing women's tears that join the tears of God in finding an alternative vision of the Deliverer God.

Chapter 3 focuses on the metaphor of God as Mother. Although the rawness of the tragedy has dissipated, this metaphor is still situated within the exile. We shall see evidence of trauma survivors looking toward the future, toward a time following the exile. The theological visions of these survivors reflect a coping strategy that seeks to make sense of what they have endured. However, in the midst of these theological visions that offer a particularly vivid account of the sovereign God who involves superpowers in God's master plan to first punish and then to save the faithful, we also see how these texts offer a window onto the pain and suffering that still lurked beneath the surface of the exilic survivors' lives. In this chapter, I reflect on the number of maternal metaphors that are used in Deutero- and Trito-Isaiah in conjunction with God's creative and liberative work. I shall argue that the metaphor of God as Mother offers a fruitful avenue to depict the possibilities of new life that Israel imagined at that stage of its journey of recovery. In a world dominated by empires that use brutal force to dominate, we shall see how female metaphors such as God as Mother in Labor (Isa. 42:13–14; 45:9–10) and God as Nurturing Mother (Isa. 49:14–15; 66:10–13) draw on values of comfort and care that may offer an opportunity to develop a different vision of the Deliverer God. Moreover, as will be seen, this maternal metaphor was well suited to address the ambiguities and continuing challenges faced by Israel in the period after the exile.

Chapter 4 introduces the metaphor of God as Midwife as it occurs in two psalms (Ps. 22:9–10; 71:6) in conjunction with the Deliverer God. Employing the connotations of a midwife who pulls a baby from the womb, thereby giving life to a child who might have died together with its mother if it stayed in the womb, the psalmist gives new significance to what it means to say that God is a Deliverer God. This chapter will also focus on the way in which these psalms of lament reflect the individual's struggle to come to grips with severe pain. However, these individual psalms could also be reinterpreted collectively in the post-exilic period to reflect the suffering of Israel as a whole. Read in this way, the psalms that employ the metaphor of God as Midwife in conjunction with the Deliverer God offer a remarkable example of the process of dealing with tragedy. We shall see, for example, how memories of past trauma break into the present experience; how the psalmist fluctuates between despair and hope for the future. Dealing honestly with the past, these psalms show glimpses of reconnection; that is, evidence of moving into the future.

In conclusion, I shall consider the implications of viewing the Deliverer God in terms of the female metaphors of God as Mourner, Mother, and Midwife—particularly the way in which these metaphors may shape the actions of contemporary believers who inevitably find themselves living in the already as well as the not-yet of God's deliverance; residing in the Land of Limbo (also known as Betwixt-and-Between). I shall show how these images work together to help create a sense of God's delivering presence in the midst of those times when liberation in the traditional sense of the word seems to be nowhere on the horizon.

It is my hope that this book will offer readers the opportunity to take a fresh look at one of the most central metaphors for God. By challenging harmful appropriations of the metaphor of God as Deliverer (the destroying, punishing, violent God) and by stretching our imaginations in light of the muted voices in the biblical text and the world to consider other aspects of this metaphor (the nurturing, supporting, caregiving God), may this book help to create a space for dealing critically and creatively with the biblical text, so as to allow for the emergence of divine metaphors that are truly liberating and transformative.

Chapter 2

God as Mourner

MOURNING WOMEN

I became interested in the image of the mourning or wailing woman almost by accident. While exploring the fascinating image of the God who weeps in Jeremiah 8:21–9:1 [MT 8:21–23]—a divine image that emerged from the very midst of the trauma of the exile, I found, just a few verses later, the image of the wailing women or "keeners,"[1] whom God summons to sing a dirge:

> Thus says the LORD of hosts:
>
> Consider, and call for the mourning women to come;
>   send for the skilled women to come;
> let them quickly raise a dirge over us,
>   so that our eyes may run down with tears,
>   and our eyelids flow with water.

For a sound of wailing is heard from Zion:
    "How we are ruined!
    We are utterly shamed,
because we have left the land,
    because they have cast down our dwellings."

Hear, O women, the word of the LORD,
    and let your ears receive the word of his mouth;
teach to your daughters a dirge,
    and each to her neighbor a lament.
                (Jer. 9:17–20 [MT 16–19])

This compelling image in Jeremiah 9 brought to mind a number of images of wailing women that captured, for me, something of the power of tears cried by women as an evocative metaphor for God. The first image comes from a book called *The Secret Life of Bees* by Sue Monk Kidd.[2] Set during the Civil Rights Struggle in the United States in the 1960s, the book tells the story of Lily, a young white girl, and her journey in search of her mother, who died when Lily was very young. Lily and her travel companion, Rosaleen, arrive at the home of a formidable black family of bee keepers, the sisters August, May, and June. Here, the girls encounter the "wailing wall" that May built. The wall functions as a symbol of all the sadness in the world. Little scraps of paper tucked into the cracks contain May's heartfelt laments, scrawled reminders of terrible injustices. One scrap of paper reads, "Birmingham, Sept. 15, four little angels dead." May regularly goes out to cry at the wall, whenever "all the heavy feelings she carries around" overwhelm her. As her sister August recounts, "It seems like the only thing that helps her." For May, the wall thus becomes a concrete means of dealing with her suffering.[3]

This image of the "wailing wall" is reminiscent of the Wailing Wall, the only remaining part of the Temple in Jerusalem, where people have gathered for centuries to mourn and to wedge prayers, written on small scraps of paper, into the cracks in the wall. A photograph taken in 1927 of women lamenting at the Wailing Wall serves as a powerful reminder of how the tears of these mourners may function as an active form of resistance.[4] This photograph reminded me of another group of women, members of the so-called "Black Sash": white South African women who stood silently, tearfully, and resolutely in public places, wearing black sashes, to protest against the injustice of apartheid. Nelson Mandela, former President of South Africa, has called these women "the conscience of the white nation."[5] Though their resistance occurred in silence, their witness was that of wailing women.

In Jeremiah 9, the wailing women are minor figures who appear only once. Consequently, they have not received much attention against the backdrop of the grand narrative of judgment and destruction that plays itself out in the book of Jeremiah. However, these barely audible voices play an important role in reshaping our understanding of the Deliverer God. In this chapter, I consider the rhetorical effect of God weeping in reaction to the suffering that Israel experienced at the hand of the Babylonian Empire. I shall argue that the image of the mourning or wailing women in Jeremiah 9:17–20 [MT 16–19] is of vital importance for understanding the way in which Judah dealt with this trauma. The wailing women's tears, which represent the depth of the community's emotion in the face of extreme trauma, are closely connected to the tears of God in Jeremiah 8:21–23 [MT 8:21-9:1]—to the extent that we can say God's tears are embodied in those of the wailing women. I propose that this metaphor of God as Wailing Woman or Mourner offers interpretative possibilities for developing an alternative understanding of God as Deliverer. Finally, I shall consider the implications of the metaphor of the Divine Mourner in terms of our own responsibility to serve as God's partners in a deeply wounded world.

TERROR ALL AROUND

"Terror is all around." There is hardly a better way to describe the devastating events brought about by the invasion of the Babylonian Empire than this recurring phrase (Jer. 20:14; 46:5; 49:29). The series of attacks by the mighty Babylonians in the years between 597 and 587 BCE resulted in the forced removal of a significant percentage of the Judean population to Babylon, and culminated in the violent destruction of the city of Jerusalem and the Temple. From these anguished times we find in the book of Jeremiah the first raw, poetic expressions of a people struggling to come to terms with the "terror all around."

In Jeremiah 4:23–26, for example, we watch as the prophet's world spirals into primordial chaos, the "waste and void" (Hebrew, *tōhû - wabōhû*) of which we read in Genesis 1:2. The prophet repeats the phrase "I looked" four times, so that the reader witnesses through the prophet's eyes a world that is steadily falling into complete disarray: the earth is "waste and void"; the heavens are dark, a reversal of God's first act of creation in Genesis 1:3 ("let there be light"); the mountains, the prime symbol of immovable strength, are shaking. This apocalyptic scenario ends with the observation that there is no one left; even the birds of the air have fled. Cities have been destroyed, and the once fruitful land has turned into a desert. In another series of shocking images, Death is personified, creeping through the windows, entering the palaces, indiscriminately leaving its mark on young and old, male and female, rich and poor (Jer. 9:21 [MT 20]). And in verse 22 [MT 21] a horrible image of human corpses falling "like dung upon the open field, like sheaves behind the reaper" serves as an ironic reversal of agricultural activity. Instead of yielding life-giving produce, the land will be strewn with corpses.

The prophet's response to this shocking reality is powerfully expressed in Jeremiah 4:19:

> My anguish, my anguish! I writhe in pain!
>   Oh, the walls of my heart!
> My heart is beating wildly;
>   I cannot keep silent;
> for I hear the sound of the trumpet,
>   the alarm of war.
> Disaster overtakes disaster,
>   the whole land is laid waste.
> Suddenly my tents are destroyed,
>   my curtains in a moment.

The prophet's raw emotion in the face of impending doom expresses a first response to a disaster that will extend far beyond the initial event. Flora Keshgegian describes the impact of trauma as "world shaking and world shattering. . . . It is like Humpty Dumpty falling off the wall. No one can put all the pieces together again, at least not without visible signs of rupture."[6]

Jeremiah's theological formulations emerge out of what Louis Stulman calls "the rubble of the fallen world." Stulman points out that in the book of Jeremiah we encounter the "utter collapse and disintegration of all existing social and symbolic categories."[7] The prophet is seeking to sculpt new theological formulations that may play some part in the survivors' efforts to pick up the remnants of their lives.[8]

In the first part of Jeremiah, two metaphors for God play a significant role in the prophet's theological attempt to make sense of the terror all around: God as Aggrieved Husband who acts out in fury against his wife, Judah (Jer. 2–3), and the God as Architect of War[9] who causes large-scale cataclysmic destruction by means of his instrument, the Babylonian Empire (Jer. 4–9). Both these metaphors work within the Deuteronomistic framework of retribution, according to which God is justified in punishing Judah for its grievous sins. Perhaps because of the chaos inflicted by the Babylonian attacks, the prophet is reasserting this framework with even greater fervor in order to maintain some sense of order. In Jeremiah 9:13–16 [MT 12–15] the link between Judah's actions and God's actions are especially clear. It is because the people have disregarded God's law and followed the Baals (vv. 13–14 [MT 12–13]) that God is pronouncing the following judgment upon Judah:

> I am feeding this people with wormwood, and giving them poisonous water to drink. I will scatter them among nations that neither they nor their ancestors have known; and I will send the sword after them, until I have consumed them. (Jer. 9:15–16 [MT 14–15])

In a dramatic reversal of the metaphor of the God who provides food and drink—a central metaphor in the collective memory of Israel—God will offer bitter, poisonous substances that do not give life but bring death (v. 15 [MT 14]). This terrible image becomes a symbol of the destruction and the dispersion of Judah outlined in verse 16 [MT 15].

For modern readers, these divine metaphors create several difficulties. Feminist theologians have shown how a metaphor of God as Abusive Spouse may not only reinforce negative gender stereotypes but also contribute to an assumption that the Bible condones violence against women.[10] Furthermore, the metaphor of God as a Mighty Warrior who does not hesitate to destroy people's lives and the land that they inhabit has disconcerting consequences in today's context of violence and bloodshed. As I noted in chapter 1 of this book, these metaphors and the underlying retributive system that explain the tragedy and terrible human anguish in terms of punishment may actually cause more problems than they solve in contemporary situations of exile and suffering.

Attempts to find appropriate ways to speak about God in contexts of severe trauma is evident in the Jewish theology that emerged during and after the Holocaust. The Holocaust led people to question the existence or the relevance of God. If one believes that God was responsible for the incomprehensible suffering of the Holocaust, how can one continue to worship this cruel, cold, and punishing Deity?[11] Alternatively, if one posits that God stood by helplessly as the tragedy played itself out, what does this say about God's ability to effect change? In both instances, the question remains: Will God survive the aftermath of the trauma?[12] Will the survivors of extreme trauma simply turn away from this seemingly uncaring or impotent God and seek other ways to recover from their past?

AND YET

And yet . . . in the midst of the prevailing discourse in Jeremiah, which views the exile as Judah's rightful punishment that God has either allowed or orchestrated, one finds another image of God, a glimpse of a radically different relationship to terrifying events and their consequences. The dominant story line—God as Aggrieved Husband and God as Architect of War—is interrupted by the image of the prophet/God who cries a fountain of tears.

> For the hurt of my poor people I am hurt,
>   I mourn, and dismay has taken hold of me.
> Is there no balm in Gilead?
>   Is there no physician there?
> Why then has the health of my poor people
>   not been restored?
> O that my head were a spring of water,
>   and my eyes a fountain of tears,
> so that I might weep day and night
>   for the slain of my poor people!
>   (Jer. 8:21–9:1 [MT 8:21–23])

Even though the prophet has shared his anguish about the people's situation throughout the book (and some scholars take the tears in this text to be his) it is significant that the poem in 9:3 [MT 9:2] ends with the phrase "says the LORD"—an indication that the passage is part of a divine speech. Moreover, Walter Brueggemann points out that God is typically the one who uses the phrase "my people."[13] I believe that Kathleen O'Connor is right when she says that the prophet's tears merge with the tears of God, who ultimately functions as the principle speaker in the poem in 8:22–9:3 [MT 8:22-9:2].[14]

The significance of this unique image of God's tears cannot be underestimated. Its ability to inspire and give hope is evident from the way in which rabbinic interpreters have discussed it over the centuries. God's tears also became particularly significant in interpreting the Jews' terrifying experiences during the Holocaust. Herbert Levine notes that, during the last days of the Warsaw Ghetto, Rabbi Kalonymus Kalman Shapiro maintained that the people's tears were joined by those of God, who had withdrawn into the inner parts of the divine palace to weep over the Jews' suffering:

> The weeping, the pain that a person undergoes by himself, alone—they may have the effect of breaking him, of bringing him down, so that he is incapable of doing anything. But the weeping that the person does together with God—that strengthens him. . . . It is hard to rise, time and again, above the sufferings; but when one summons the courage—stretching the mind to engage in Torah and divine service—then he enters the inner chambers where God is to be found. There he weeps and wails with Him, as it were, together.[15]

The incredible power of God's tears to make a difference in human survival is imaginatively narrated in the Jewish tradition. According to the rabbis, when God remembered the suffering of God's children in exile, God dropped two tears into the ocean. The sound of these tears, heard from one end of the earth to the other, had a seismological effect, causing tremors to shake the earth (*b. Berakhot* 59a). Herbert Basser comments on this tradition as follows:

> God's love of Israel shines through his tears. The rabbis find nothing more powerful than the immensity of these tears and note their chaotic potential: the vibrations can lead to earthquakes and seismic tremors. God's tears, though controlled, and but two in number, can wreak havoc.[16]

The image of the God who weeps, with its associations of solidarity with God's people as well as the inherent power of God's tears to effect change, speaks to people in a way that few others images are able to. But beyond its ability to serve as a source of comfort and inspiration, this image of the God who weeps challenges our perceptions about the age-old question of theodicy. In the midst of violence, bloodshed, terror, and anguish, this imagery of the weeping God steers the conversation in a whole new direction: it offers the "and yet." At the very least, God's tears complicate the arguments, suggesting that descriptions of God's brute force do not sufficiently address the concerns of bruised people standing up from the rubble. As Levine formulates this alternative understanding: "A radically new view of God is present here. If God can be represented as weeping over what happened to Israel, indeed over what God made happen to Israel, then the angry, all powerful God of retribution has been dethroned."[17]

In this regard, Kathleen O'Connor argues that "the tears of God are part of the imaginative literary enterprise that ruptures theological language."[18] In contrast to the dominant story line, which justifies violence, the rupture caused by the image of the God who weeps allows for an alternative understanding of God to emerge. In the image of God's tears one sees, for the briefest of moments, the possibility of a relationship without violence. The image of the God who weeps offers an interruption that allows new possibilities for hope to emerge.[19]

A second significant point: it is the sight of the people's suffering that causes this rupture. In Jeremiah 8:22, for example, we see how God weeps *because of* the "hurt of my poor people." The reference to "my poor people" is repeated three times in these verses and frames the image of the divine tears. God's act of seeing the pain, of noticing the tears of the people, causes God to weep uncontrollably.

The first-person verbs used to identify God with the plight of Daughter Zion signal that the distance between God and the people has been bridged. Thus Jeremiah 8:21 uses variations of the root word *šbr* ("to break") to state that, as Judah is broken (*šeber*), so too is God (*hošbārtî*). It is the people's wounds that cause God's spirit to grow leaden and that cause horror to take hold of God (literally, God is "seized" [*heḥĕziqātnî*] with horror).[20]

There may be various reasons for God's tears. Throughout the book of Jeremiah, the injustices committed by the religious establishment, who did not protect the little ones and did not heed the covenant obligations of providing for the poor and vulnerable in society, are glaringly evident (Jer. 2:34; 5:28). Because the victims of social injustice are part of Daughter Judah, the wounds inflicted on Judah's body afflict God in a very personal way. As Nicholas Wolterstorff, drawing on John Calvin, argues: "to inflict injury on a fellow human being is to wound God himself; it is to cause God himself to suffer." According to Wolterstorff, if we truly believed this, "we would be much more reluctant than we are to participate in the victimizing of the poor and the oppressed and the assaulted of this world."[21] God feels the devastation of war in God's own self. The highly visible wounds inflicted on the city and her people cause deep-seated suffering for God.

Given Jeremiah's strong message of God's judgment and the people's deserved punishment, it is remarkable that God nonetheless sheds tears for these fragile people. Setting aside questions of blame, God's tears become a source of salvation. For liberation to take place, God has to feel the people's suffering. Only the weeping God can feel the people's pain; only the suffering God can help.[22] As Levine argues, "Israel chooses a God with whom it can continue to identify, namely, a God who identifies with its pain." Among the survivors in Judah there were at least some "who refused to take into their long exile the God who had so cruelly expelled them from their land."[23]

It is important to understand that the image of the God who weeps is a product of a community that, through its tears, was seeking to come to terms with its communal and individual grief. The book of Jeremiah is permeated with tears: heaven and earth mourn (Jer. 4:28), Rachel cries inconsolably for her children who are no more (Jer. 31:15–17) and, as we have seen before, the tears of the prophet merge with God's tears (Jer. 8:21–9:1 [MT 8:21–23]). It is indeed a traumatized and bereaved people who imagined their God as weeping. But perhaps one of the best examples in Jeremiah of the community's response to its trauma is the tears cried by the keener or the wailing woman.

CALLING THE KEENERS

In the Ancient Near East, as well as in certain contemporary societies, wailing women fulfill a central role in helping the community come to terms with its grief. In these cultures, women are responsible for the expression of public, corporate lament.[24] In ancient times, mourning or wailing women were groups of women who were invited to attend funerals and other somber events to lead the participants in mourning; much like a cantor or choir leads a congregation in its liturgy.[25]

Fokkelien van Dijk-Hemmes, who has studied traces of women's texts in the Hebrew Bible, argues that, even though most of the laments preserved in the Hebrew Bible can probably be attributed to male authors, the lament genre is par excellence the domain of women. One sees evidence of this in the number of texts that mention only women in connection with mourning; for example, the daughters of Israel whom David summoned to weep for Saul and Jonathan (2 Sam. 1:24) and the women of the nations that will chant laments over the "hordes of Egypt" (Ezek. 32:16–18).[26]

In Jeremiah 9:17–20 [MT 16–19], wailing women are called on to lead the people in expressions of grief in response to the national tragedy that saw the destruction of Zion. These women who are called to "raise a dirge over us" are literally called "wise women." This can also be translated as "skilled women" (Jer. 9:17 [MT 16]), suggesting that the art of mourning is a skill that has to be learned. The role of the wailing woman constituted a professional trade that required training.[27]

On the appropriate occasion (a funeral or a national tragedy like the one that forms the backdrop of Jeremiah 9), wailing women not only had to be able to draw on the reservoir of laments handed down through the generations, but they also had to adapt these laments to suit the particular needs of the current situation.[28] By means of this creative actualization of the lament tradition, the wailing women vocalized what the people needed to express. Their laments represented the community's response in the face of extreme trauma.[29] The wailing women demonstrated to the community how to react appropriately in light of the circumstances—as verse 18 [MT 17] says, "so that our eyes may run down with tears, and our eyelids flow with water."

It is significant, however, that not only those trained in the art of keening are called to wail, but all the women of Israel. God urges all the women to teach their daughters a dirge and their neighbors a lament (v. 20 [MT 19]). It seems that the sheer magnitude of the calamity called for the role of the professional keeners to be extended to all the women in the community, who needed to take an active role in helping the rest of the community to grieve.

The Therapeutic Role of Wailing Women

The wailing women fulfilled an important *therapeutic role* in society by helping it to deal with its grief.[30] The wailing women's laments and tears created a space for the people to express their emotions. By leading the community in weeping and by uttering laments or dirges, the wailing women were responsible for finding the first words to vocalize what had happened. Trauma often leaves people numb and confused, unable to express their emotions. The wailing women's tears helped the people to break through the silence toward a basic, raw vocalization of their grief. In this regard Kathleen Sands argues that the genre of the lament or "tragedy, as an aesthetic form, consigns trauma to a ritual space where rather than being silently reenacted, it is solemnly voiced and lamented."[31] Keshgegian continues: "This ritual narration may move trauma from the hidden spheres of silence. The repetition may spin slender threads of life-nourishing connection."[32]

The wailing women take the lead in naming what happened to the people when they exclaim, "How we are ruined"—the verb *šdd* has connotations of being "devastated," "dealt violently with," "despoiled," and "destroyed." The wailing women voice how the people feel "utterly ashamed" of their city, home, and temple going up in smoke, and from having the Babylonian invaders forcefully remove them from their homes and land. The wailing women voice the terrible memory of death entering their dwellings, cutting down children where they ought to be playing and young men in the spaces where they typically gather. Furthermore, the wailing women's laments narrate the obscene reality of unburied human corpses strewn like manure in the fields. By taking up this call to lament, by naming the tragic events without avoiding the pain, the wailing women lead the community in the first steps of a long journey toward healing and recovery.

Wailing Women's Role in Leading Communal Lament

The actions of the wailing women contribute significantly to the *communal nature* of lament. Grief is meant to be shared, especially when a tragedy affects the entire community. The wailing women succeed in bringing the community together in their grief. We see something of this communal response in the reference to women teaching their daughters and their neighbors to lament: in this way, they take responsibility for the fact that the whole community is involved. The astounding power of tears to cause others to join in the mourning finds poignant expression in an intriguing midrash from Lamentations Rabbah, where the tears cried by Daughter Zion (who has no one to comfort her in Lam. 1:1–2) have a remarkable effect on those who are witnessing this outpouring of grief.[33] In Lamentations Rabbah 23, Daughter Zion's lament in Jerusalem is portrayed as having an effect on a range of divine, human, and inanimate subjects:

> She [Daughter Zion] weeps and makes others to weep with her. Thus she weeps and makes the Holy One blessed be He, to weep with her for it is written, And in that day did the Lord, the God of hosts, call to weeping, and to lamentation. (Isa. 22:12)

The midrash further relates how Daughter Zion's weeping makes the ministering angels to weep with her; it makes heaven and earth to weep with her (see the proof text of Joel 2:10), as well as the mountains and hills (see the proof text of Jer. 4:24, which refers to the trembling of the mountains). Finally, her weeping makes the community of Israel to weep with her.

Referring to Daughter Zion's appearance in the book of Lamentations, Goitein suggests that she is fulfilling the role of the wailing woman in inciting others to join in lament.[34] There is a close association between the tears of the wailing women—in this instance, Daughter Zion—and the God who weeps.

Wailing Women as Witness

The wailing women can be understood with reference to the category of *witness* or *testimony* that forms a fundamental concept in trauma theory. The witness is the survivor who is left behind, tormented and bruised, yet who is still able to stand up and speak about the calamity.[35]

Writing about victims of the Holocaust, Shoshana Felman argues that the very act of bearing witness to trauma—that is, "the story of survival"—occurs "at the crossroads between life and death." The tears and laments of the wailing women as represented in literature form in Jeremiah 9 can thus be understood in terms of a testimony to what has transpired, calling on the rest of the community not to forget but to honestly and bravely name their pain. Thus the wailing women play a significant role in helping the people of Judah to come together in their grief, and so to participate in the "survival of the[ir] story."[36]

This notion of testimony is an essential part of helping others to deal with pain. Using the figure (from Camus' novel *The Plague*) of the physician who bears witness for those who died during the plague, Felman argues regarding the significance of testimony as an act of survival that

> Camus' choice of the physician as the privileged narrator and the designated witness might suggest that the capacity to witness and the act of bearing witness in themselves embody some remedial quality and belong already, in obscure ways, to the healing process.[37]

In Jeremiah 9, the wailing women are the ones who voice the community's pain, and whose laments serve as memory of what and whom were lost. Without the witness of the wailing women, the victims of the violent attacks will fade into oblivion.[38] Moreover, as Felman's example of Camus indicates, to understand the wailing women as witnesses may be a necessary step in coming to terms with the trauma and taking the first uncertain steps toward healing.

The Prophetic Role of Wailing Women

The wailing women's tears serve a *prophetic role*. S. D. Goitein, who has explored the phenomenon of wailing women in the contemporary community of Jewish women in Yemen, remarks that the women's lamenting sometimes takes the form of prophecy.[39] Goitein uses the example of a Yemenite woman who, despite her "limited social position, expressed in her poetry public opinion of the events of the day"—much like the editorial in the daily newspaper.[40]

The wailing women in Jeremiah fulfill a similar function when their tears give powerful, visible expression to the fact that everything is not as it should be. As the prophet challenged the community by saying, you say "peace, peace, when there is no peace" (Jer. 6:14; 8:11), the wailing women challenge complacency that ignores the many social injustices threatening the well-being of their society as a whole.[41] Being summoned by God to raise up a lament and to involve the community by teaching their daughters and neighbors, the wailing women serve as God's spokespersons, as the people's conscience in protesting against the wrongs in their world. Receiving the word from God's mouth (v. 20 [MT 19]), the wailing women call on the people to live in justice so that others may live as well.

In this regard, the wailing women's weeping can be viewed as an act of resistance. When we consider the Babylonian invasion and exile in terms of conquest (see the "god, gold, and glory" principle that constitutes the driving forces of later empires), the wailing women's tears and laments vocalize the extent of the brokenness and injustice of their situation. With little real power to effect change, the women's tears become a way to resist the empire's brutality. By means of this very limited act of resistance, their tears also become a powerful sign of hope that contributes to the broader community's will to survive.

DIVINE WAILING WOMAN

It is interesting to note that God's tears precede those of the wailing women in Jeremiah 9. This chapter, in which the keening women are summoned to sing their lament, begins with the dramatic portrayal of the God who weeps. God's tears initiate the women's mourning. God fulfills the role of wailing woman by initiating the lament and by teaching the keening women their skill so that they can, in turn, teach others. By summoning the mourners in verse 20 [MT 19], God is leading the people in mourning. In this way God is providing the wailing women with the cue that now is the right time to lament. The messenger formula—"thus says the Lord" (v. 20 [MT 19])—indicates that the divine word is coming to the wailing women, who are implored to "hear the word of the Lord" and to receive the teaching from God's mouth (v. 22 [MT 21]) (see also the divine summons to mourn in Jer. 4:8; 6:26). Viewed in this way, God becomes a Wailing or Mourning Woman.

A text-critical problem in verse 10 [MT 9] offers an intriguing perspective on the notion of the Divine Wailing Woman's call to lament. If one chooses to follow the Masoretic text, God is the subject of the sentence, "I will take up weeping and wailing" (see the NIV translation). However, if one opts for the Greek and Syriac versions (see the NRSV translation), the verse reads as a plural imperative: "Take up weeping and wailing"—denoting a call to the community to lament. Terence Fretheim argues that the Masoretic reading powerfully expresses God's suffering over the calamity that befell the people. However, the translation that draws on the Greek version suggests that God's summons to the community to take up wailing and weeping implies "a divine pathos to be voiced by the community."[42] I suggest that one keeps these diverse readings together to forge a connection between God's own grief, as expressed in 8:21–9:1 [MT 21–23] and that of the wailing women, who lead the community in their grief (9:17–20 [MT 16–19]). As the Divine Mourner, God calls on the people to weep and wail along with God.[43]

To view God as Wailing Woman or Mourner helps us to gain insight into those most devastating of times when all that was to be seen was terror all around, when it seemed nearly impossible to sing songs of liberation proclaiming that "God is our Deliverer!" Except for what is known as the "Little Book of Consolation" (Jer. 30–33), there seems to be little hope of liberation in the book of Jeremiah. When the wailing women enter upon the stage, there seems to be no response, no hope for recovery, no "they lived happily ever after" moments that the people are craving so dearly. However, in the midst of these utterly desperate circumstances, the wailing women's bold raising of their voices in lament helps the community to deal with its trauma. In terms of the overall objective of this book, viewing God's tears in terms of the female metaphor of the wailing woman offers intriguing possibilities for reshaping the traditional meaning of God as Deliverer: deliverance not associated with violence.

The metaphor of the Divine Mourner is closely associated with the survival of the people. In what proves to be a bold act of faith, the survivors dare to imagine a God whose tears call on the community to start naming that which they have lost. It is remarkable that, in response to the terrible tragedy, the people are able to discern a divine image that could aid their recovery from the traumatizing events.

The process of immersing oneself in the painful memories of devastation and loss is exceedingly painful.[44] However, the very act of breaking the silence and acknowledging the pain reflects the people's yearning for new life, which can indeed be described in terms of salvation, healing, liberation, and redemption. The tears of the Divine Mourner thus offer the first step in a prolonged process of dealing with the ongoing effects of severe trauma. O'Connor argues that the memories of trauma "cut through the blockages: the numbness, the memories of violence and loss, the bitter realization that life will never recover its previous shape. . . . By plunging its readers deep into memories of disaster, it acknowledges them and brings them into the light. Hope, then, can be more than wishful thinking, more than another form of denial or a naïve dream. Like some preaching, these hard words make room for hope to reside, to set up house and do its work of rebuilding."[45]

Moreover, redemption is intrinsically connected to survivors' ability to rebuild a life that includes honestly and courageously naming the hurts of the past as well as claiming a life beyond the disaster.[46] This process of reclaiming life is by no means a simple, uncomplicated process, but it is deeply rooted in the challenges of the survivors' everyday reality. As Keshgegian argues,

> Redemption is in history even though there is much pain and loss in history. The world and history remain ambiguous spaces, constructed by processes of power welded into foundations held firm, except for those historical earthquakes that cause cracks and occasional splintering. There is no true certainty among those who remember suffering only a learning to dance amid the tremors, to move with grace and hope and "with no extraordinary power, reconstitute the world" (Adrienne Rich). Though the world is dangerous, it is only by remembering in the face of the danger that new life can be fully claimed.[47]

The metaphor of God as Wailing Woman grounds God's tears in the community's reality—the wailing women find themselves deeply enmeshed in the calamity, thoroughly engaged in the current events. As Tova Gamliel notes in an essay on the wailing culture of elderly Yemenite-Jewish women, the communal performance of the wailing women blurs the distinction between them and the audience, establishing a symbiotic relationship between the various participants.[48] The metaphor of the Divine Mourner is an example of incarnational theology—God enters into solidarity with those reeling from the trauma—modeling something of the "withness" that Flora Keshgegian proposes.[49] In contrast to divine imagery that places God in an abusive and violent relationship with the people, the metaphor of God as Wailing Woman sets God in the midst of the believers' painful reality. It depicts a God who is part of the community; who weeps together with the community; who is wounded with the same wounds that afflict the people.

God's solidarity with the community in the midst of a reality where few signs of any immediate relief are to be found (in Jeremiah we read that the looming exile was to last at least 70 years—for most people, spanning the whole of their lives) changes the way we think about the confession that God is our Liberator God. In this regard, to imagine God as Mourner or Wailing Woman, weeping and mourning as loudly as the women leading the people in their grief, complicates the traditional understanding of God as Warrior and Aggrieved Husband that dominates much of the biblical witness and especially the prophetic discourse. The Divine Mourner, embodied in the wailing women of Israel, opens up new possibilities of liberation because it shows that, even though there may not be any immediate relief from the terror all around, God is in the midst of the people's suffering and devastation; God is weeping *with* them.

This alternative metaphor of God as Wailing Woman challenges theological constructions that explain God in terms of divine retribution, which have dominated much of biblical interpretation. Ultimately, this dominant discourse forms, as Stulman puts it, "a closed network in which conduct and condition are inexorably correlated and in which God is tamed and domesticated."[50] According to Stulman, we find in the book of Jeremiah a similar process to what is happening in the book of Job, where the reader is presented with a "wild and undomesticated God who refuses to be imprisoned by any closed system."[51] In the image of the Divine Mourner, God is perceived as being profoundly involved in suffering, sharing the pain experienced by the victims of trauma.

The image of God as Mourner also raises all sorts of questions regarding the gendered nature of tears. Even though there are many male figures in the Bible who lament or weep (e.g., Joseph weeps when he sees his brother Benjamin in Gen. 45:14; David weeps over his son Absalom in 2 Sam. 19:1; and Jesus weeps in John 11:35), the role of the keener was most often associated with women.[52] Is it because, throughout the ages, mothers and wives who have lost their children and husbands in war have wept over their loved ones?[53] Or is it because women are more likely to be excluded from the "structured public life carried on by and for men," and so they are more inclined to be associated with "speech-disrupting tears"?[54] Regardless of the reason for the gendered nature of tears, in the biblical tradition, Rachel—the wife of Jacob, who became "Israel"—serves as the quintessential figure of grief. In Jeremiah 31:15–17, Rachel weeps for her children "who are no more" and refuses to be comforted. Rachel, the woman who knew the anguish of barrenness and then died giving birth to her second son, serves as the symbol of the Jewish mothers whose children have been carried off into exile, ghettos, or concentration camps. In her grief, Rachel also becomes the symbol of mothers who weep over the senseless suffering of their children (see also how Jer. 31:15 is cited in Matt. 2:18 in the context of Herod's command to slay all the baby boys in Bethlehem).[55]

To think of the God who weeps in terms of a wailing or mourning woman offers a unique perspective on the nature of God and provides female imagery for the Divine that balances male imagery. To view God in terms of a woman weeping over the devastation that befell her community strongly challenges the portrayal of God as a mighty male figure who plays war games with the nations or who beats up his insolent wife—images that have dominated many interpretations of Jeremiah.[56]

The metaphor of God as Mourner finally offers us the opportunity to develop an alternative understanding of power. Traditionally, women held little power in the public sphere. However, the wailing women were summoned in times when the traditional power structures of the community had fallen into disarray. In a time of crisis, the wailing women had the power to bring the community together in their grief. Thus, wailing women's power was not power in the traditional sense; nevertheless, their tears had the power to help survivors deal with their trauma and to resist violence by raising their voices in protest against the injustice of the terror all around.

Similarly, the image of God as Mourner resonates with biblical imagery of power in vulnerability, e.g., Deutero-Isaiah's use of suffering servant imagery, and God as Mother in Labor (to be discussed in the next chapter), culminating in the image of the Crucified God on the cross.[57] The God who weeps, the God who is wounded because of what is happening to God's children and the world they inhabit, the God who is embodied in the female metaphor of the Wailing Woman challenges the portrayal of God as the strong and mighty Liberator God and offers an "other" God: a God whose liberating compassion and love are stronger than God's anger and judgment.

LOOKING AT THE WORLD THROUGH TEARS

Envisioning God's tears in terms of the female figure of the Wailing Woman has significant ethical implications for a world that in many ways is still as broken as it was in the time when the original image was introduced. Weeping has a powerful effect on the way we look at the world and at one another. As Nicholas Wolterstorff said after his son died in a mountaineering accident, "I shall look at the world through tears. Perhaps I shall see things that dry-eyed I could not."[58] The fact that God is fulfilling the role of Wailing Woman or Divine Mourner, calling on the community to weep, will affect the way people see the world and live their lives.

Tears have the powerful ability to break down barriers. Tears, particularly tears of compassion, can bring about healing where there used to be hatred or distrust. Kathleen O'Connor writes, "Tears heal because they bring people together in suffering, and reveal them to one another in their vulnerability."[59]

I am reminded of a powerful scene in the film *Cry the Beloved Country* (1995), based on the eponymous book that for a very long time was banned in my home country, South Africa. The film tells the story of two elderly men, a black pastor and a white farmer. One day, their lives become inextricably intertwined when the pastor's son kills the farmer's son in faraway Johannesburg during a break-in that went terribly wrong. Both the farmer and the pastor are devastated. The pastor tells his friend, "I do not know what it is these days, but I cry all the time." The farmer does not cry; he is furious that his son's life has been taken away so violently. The pastor's and the farmer's lives intersect in court when they hear the pastor's son receive the death penalty. Later they encounter each other again during a rainstorm, when the farmer seeks shelter in the pastor's church. In this little church, with its dilapidated, leaking roof, the pastor's tears wash away the animosity and anger between the two men and they can meet each other in a new way.

When considering the ethical implications of the tears of the God who weeps as embodied in the wailing women of the community, it is important to consider that the tears of the Divine Mourner included the victims of the social injustice perpetrated and the devastation caused by the Babylonian Empire. As Wailing Woman in the community, God sheds tears that evoke response and teach the community to see the wounds of the victims of social violations. God's tears are an indication that God has not given up on the community; God summons the wailing women, teaching the community how to lament injustice. The tears of God and the wailing women challenged the Judean community at the time of the exile—and communities ever since—to have the same broken heart as God and to work for change wherever change is possible.

The call to work toward justice, peace, and reconciliation is rooted in God's pathos. According to Nicholas Wolterstorff, "The call to justice is the call to avoid wounding God; the call to eliminate injustice is the call to alleviate divine suffering."[60] The appropriate response to seeing God's tears, to hearing God's weeping, is to respond to the Wailing Woman's call by letting "our wounds bleed" and "our eyes tear."[61] Justice is thus rooted in our ability to weep with God. Lamenting should lead to change, liberation, healing, and reconciliation.[62] As Denise Ackermann writes, "No reconciliation is possible without repentance. The call to lament is an appeal to all, both the victims and to the repentant perpetrators of suffering, to engage in public acts of mourning which will enable true reconciliation and healing to take place."[63]

It is also important to consider that God's tears are a protest against violence. Bracketing questions of blame, God's tears suggest that God sees the plight of the victims who are suffering at the hands of the powerful. Together with the tears of the wailing women in the community, God's tears say no to the brute force of the imperial powers, calling on the community to find ways to resist violence. Thus Kathleen O'Connor describes tears as "a political language that opposes the language of power."[64] O'Connor employs a story told by C. S. Song that artfully describes the power of tears as part of people's political resistance in China. Song tells the story of a Chinese woman whose husband is violently taken away on his wedding day to serve as a human sacrifice for ensuring the successful completion of the Great Wall of China. Later, the woman travels to the wall where her husband's bones are buried. There she begins to cry inconsolably. Song writes, "Truly astonishing the power of Lady Meng's tears! . . . Her wailing must have moved the firmament of heaven, shaken the foundations of the earth. Her crying must have stirred all 'living souls' . . . to rally behind her. And an incredible thing happened. The Wall, that invincible Wall, the Wall that embodied brutal power and naked authority, collapsed and yielded up her husband's bones."[65]

The tears of the people serve as an important—quite often the only— tool to counter injustice. The tears of God, as embodied in the wailing women, call on us to resist those instances where contemporary manifestations of the empire abuse their power—be it in instances of war and genocide, or where big business and oil companies abuse their power, or where unjust governments trample upon whoever is in their way.

Another intriguing example of weeping as a means of political resistance comes from a song called "Weeping." A white South African, Dan Heymann, wrote this song of protest against the cast iron wall of apartheid, which was held in place by the regime of the then State President P. W. Botha, and the compulsory military service that enforced it:

I knew a man who lived in fear
It was huge, it was angry, it was drawing near
Behind his house, a secret place
Was the shadow of the demon he could never face
He built a wall of steel and flame
And men with guns, to keep it tame
Then standing back, he made it plain
That the nightmare would never ever rise again
But the fear and the fire and the guns remain
   It doesn't matter now
   It's over anyhow
   He tells the world that it's sleeping
   But as the night came round
   I heard its lonely sound
   It wasn't roaring, it was weeping
And then one day the neighbors came
They were curious to know about the smoke and flame
They stood around outside the wall
But of course there was nothing to be heard at all

"My friends," he said, "We've reached our goal
The threat is under firm control
As long as peace and order reign
I'll be damned if I can see a reason to explain
Why the fear and the fire and the guns remain."[66]

The remarkable thing about this song is that, in the midst of the violence and the guns that squelch opposition, one hears the sound of weeping: "a lonely sound" that is not "roaring." The final stanza of the song suggests that the power structures are still firmly in place, seemingly oblivious to the protestors' tears. However, history has proven once again that an empire's hold does not last. The weeping was heard.[67] The Soweto String Quartet's recording of this song includes a fascinating detail that makes a powerful theological claim: one hears a single violin playing the tune of *Nkosi Sikelel' iAfrika*—"God bless Africa."[68] The violin is like the sound of weeping rising in protest against injustice, or a prayer to the God who weeps with us.

Weeping does not automatically lead to positive action, to uniting people in their pain, or to working for justice. One of the greatest challenges for those who have fallen victim to violence such as Judah experienced in the devastating attacks by the Babylonian Empire is to avoid a situation where weeping and lamenting turn into revenge. In the instance of Psalm 137, we clearly see how the focus has shifted from blaming God to blaming the perpetrators.[69] Thus, the bitter weeping of the trauma survivors by the rivers of Babylon ends with fantasies of revenge, of bashing the heads of the enemies' babies against the rocks.

Regarding the visions of vengeance in the book of Nahum that revel in the Assyrian enemy's demise, David Garber warns that trauma survivors engage in false testimony "that tends toward passing victimization from the real enemy to an innocent bystander." In such a scenario, in order to rebuild their lives in the face of tragedy, groups may engage in "misdirected vengeance" that can traumatize another innocent group of people.[70]

In light of this reality, the tears with which God urges the community to weep become even more important. Weeping in community, as well as weeping across communities, may offer the connection that brings people together in their grief and prevents them from succumbing to fantasies and actions of revenge. It is by remembering the complex stories of suffering and survival, without reinforcing a sense of victimization or seeking vindication, that we may move toward a future filled with new possibilities of life and of love.[71]

Pumla Gobodo-Madikizela, a psychologist who served on the Truth and Reconciliation Commission, tells a gripping story of the meeting between Eugene de Kock (the commanding officer of the state-sanctioned death squads in South Africa, who was responsible for the disappearance and death of numerous antiapartheid activists) and the widow of one of his victims, Mrs. Pearl Faku. In an interview after their meeting, the bereaved widow said,

> I couldn't control my tears. I could hear him, but I was overwhelmed by emotion, and I was just nodding as a way of saying, yes, I forgive you. I hope that when he sees our tears, he knows that they are not only tears for our husbands but tears for him as well. . . . I would like to hold him by the hand, and show him there is a future and that he can still change.[72]

Gobodo-Madikizela argues that "the possibility of making an emphatic connection with someone who has victimized us" is rooted in a shared sense of connectedness, of being able to reach out and tell the other, "I can feel the pain you feel for having caused me pain." According to Gobodo-Madikizela, it is this ability of people to forge a connection that "makes it possible for enemies to connect in a way that might otherwise seem unimaginable."[73]

Finally, the call of the Divine Mourner to take up mourning and weeping paradoxically serves as a symbol of hope. As Pamela Scalise argues, "the way of weeping" is the only road that leads to healing and restoration.[74] In Jeremiah 31:7–22, it is significant that the promises of new life and restoration are addressed to those who have heeded the call of the wailing women. In verses 8–9, for instance, we find God's promise:

> See, I am going to bring them from the land of the north,
>   and gather them from the farthest parts of the earth,
> among them the blind and the lame,
>   those with child and those in labor, together;
>   a great company, they shall return here.
> With weeping they shall come,
>   and with consolations I will lead them back,
> I will let them walk by brooks of water,
>   in a straight path in which they shall not stumble;
> for I have become a father to Israel,
>   and Ephraim is my firstborn.

As the title of Walter Brueggemann's essay "Faith at the *Nullpunkt*" (at the "ground zero" points of Judah's history—a term that he used some time before 9/11) indicates, in the Hebrew Bible faith is the remarkable, though often almost incomprehensible, act of believing in a life beyond the immediate circumstances, no matter how impossible it seems.[75] The tears of the trauma survivors, the communal action of weeping together, are signs that those who are weeping and wailing are keeping on living, keeping on hoping for a new life to come. Keshgegian describes this very act of existence in the midst of ongoing trauma as "a creative practice in the moment, for the sake of survival, and a continuing to live with hope for redemption."[76]

Chapter 3

God as Mother

MOTHERS

As I was working on the remarkable cluster of maternal metaphors in Deutero- and Trito-Isaiah, metaphors that offer some intriguing perspectives on God as Deliverer, many personal images of mothers came to mind. My wonderful mother, grandmother, mother-in-law, and Doktormutter all have shaped and enriched my life. I was also drawn to stories and images of mothers who have nurtured not only their own children but whomever crossed their paths throughout their lives.[1]

One visual image that in particular captures this self-giving and nurturing aspect of motherhood is a 1942 lithograph by the German artist Käthe Kollwitz, called "Seed Corn Must Not Be Ground." Kollwitz's portrayal of an older woman, perhaps a mother, who protects the "seed corn"—symbolic of the future of the human race—is a visual protest against the waste of war. The defiant woman is desperately sheltering three young children, not necessarily her own offspring, who represent war's most vulnerable victims. Erika Langmuir argues that, even though this lithograph is designed "as a protest against the drafting of very young boys into the German army" by a woman who herself had lost a son in World War I, this print "could just as easily represent victims of German aggression, German victims of Allied bombing, or the women and children of any genocidal war in history."[2]

As I shall show in the concluding chapter of this book, Melissa Raphael uses these nurturing and protective actions of mothers rooted in "a capacity to bend over and cover, stroke, warm, feed, clean, lift and hold the other" to depict "an embodied resistance to Auschwitz which had institutionalized the exposure, breakage and waste of bodies." In Auschwitz, "mothers had mothered daughters; daughters, mothers; sisters, sisters; friends, friends; and mothers, other mothers. That mothering was in many senses futile and pitifully ineffectual to the scale of loss, terror, and deprivation." However, as Raphael argues, in none of the memoirs of Holocaust survivors she consulted, "were [mothering's] comforts incidental or peripheral to meaning and hope, then or now."[3]

These contemporary portrayals of women protecting their children offer a powerful image as one explores the role of the maternal imagery used in Deutero-Isaiah to describe a people's valiant attempts to survive the deeply traumatic events of war and state-sponsored acts of terror.

DEUTERO-ISAIAH AS SURVIVAL LITERATURE

If ever there was a time that Israel was in need of a Deliverer, it was in the wake of the cataclysmic events of the Babylonian exile. In the previous chapter we saw a heart-wrenching display of the raw emotions evoked by the sheer terror of seeing one's city going up in smoke, witnessing the ravaging of the land and the destruction of the Temple, and dealing with the tremendous loss of life and autonomy. The anguished cries of physically and emotionally traumatized survivors in books like Jeremiah and Lamentations represent both those taken into exile as well as those left amid the city's ruins, as they painfully came to terms with the loss of everything that had given life significance.

We also know that the tragedy of the Babylonian exile had a marked effect on the way people believed. Together with the tumbling down of the Temple walls, people's religious beliefs were seriously challenged. The airtight theological constructions of the past suddenly seemed just as feeble as the once sturdy walls of the Temple. Shaken in their naivety, people wondered what had happened to the once powerful God who was professed in psalm and story as the Deliverer God who had freed their ancestors from Egypt and who had led Israel through the wilderness into the promised land. The devastation caused by the Babylonian army catapulted the believers into a theological crisis, raising serious doubts whether it was possible to keep on believing in the Deliverer God of their past. Emotional damage and the effects of trauma may extend well beyond the initial traumatic event.[4] In this regard, the words of the sixth-century prophet known as Deutero-Isaiah can be described as survival literature that helped the exiles to face their trauma and to move into the future in a constructive way. In the rhetorically powerful discourse of Isaiah 40–55, one sees how the prophet uses innovative strategies to provide the survivors with a new theological framework to "jolt them into a new and creative way of interpreting their life."[5] One of these strategies is the marvelous blend of tradition and innovation that plays itself out throughout the prophetic discourse of Deutero-Isaiah. Close to each other, we find the call to remember the things of old (Isa. 46:8–9) as well as the call *not* to remember the former things (Isa. 43:18). This dialectic reflects the intrinsic tension between continuity and creativity that is at the heart of the theological tradition. The challenges brought about by the Babylonian exile were responsible for what Paul Hanson calls "an explosion of new meaning" as traditional imagery was subjected to "considerable experimentation and innovation."[6] Thus the prophet picks up earlier traditions, such as God as Deliverer, and interrupts this metaphor with a variety of compelling images that subvert, challenge, broaden, and enrich the original formulation. The prophet draws on the memory of past formulations but leads the way to a new understanding in order to convince the broken exiles of an alternative reality in which they may think in new and hopeful ways about the significance of God's deliverance.

DISJUNCTIVE METAPHORS

One striking example of this tendency to interrupt traditional formulations with new meaning is the female metaphors used to describe the Deliverer God in Isaiah 40–66. In four instances, the metaphors of God as Mother in Labor and God as Nurturing Mother are used respectively in close proximity to more well-known metaphors for God, thus providing sparks of new meaning regarding God's liberation. In Isaiah 42:13–14, the metaphor of God as Mother in Labor is paired with the metaphor of the Divine Warrior:

> The LORD goes forth like a soldier,
>   like a warrior he stirs up his fury;
> he cries out, he shouts aloud,
>   he shows himself mighty against his foes.
> For a long time I have held my peace,
>   I have kept still and restrained myself;
> now I will cry out like a woman in labor,
>   I will gasp and pant
>   (Isa. 42:13–14)

The Ancient Near Eastern metaphor of the Divine Warrior is often used in conjunction with the metaphors of God as Creator and Liberator (e.g., Isa. 51:9–10; Ps. 74:12–14; Isa. 27:1). But in Isaiah 42:14 the prophet introduces an unexpected metaphor that describes the Deliverer God as Mother in Labor[7] whose cries merge with those of the shouting warrior. These two metaphors work together to depict God's powerful ability to bring forth not only victory over enemies but also new life.

In Isaiah 45:9–11 the same metaphor (God as Mother in Labor) is used to very different effect:

> Woe to you who strive with your Maker,
>   earthen vessels with the potter!
> Does the clay say to the one who fashions it, "What are you making"?
>   or "Your work has no handles"?
> Woe to anyone who says to a father, "What are you begetting?"
>   or to a woman, "With what are you in labor?"
>   (Isa. 45:9–10)

This time, the metaphor of a Mother in Labor is used for God in conjunction with the metaphors of God as Father who sires a child and God as Artisan who shapes a pot from clay. Sarah Dille argues that the point of comparison among these metaphors is their respective abilities to create something new. These metaphors work together to convey to Israel the radical idea that Cyrus, the king of the Persian Empire—who is called God's "anointed" (Isa. 45:1) and God's "shepherd" (Isa.

44:28)—will be the means by which God will create a new future for Israel.[8]

In Isaiah 49:13–15 God is portrayed as a nurturing mother who comforts her child:

> Sing for joy, O heavens, and exult, O earth;
>   break forth, O mountains, into singing!
> For the LORD has comforted his people,
>   and will have compassion on his suffering ones.
> But Zion said, "The LORD has forsaken me,
>   my Lord has forgotten me."
> Can a woman forget her nursing child,
>   or show no compassion for the child of her womb?
> Even these may forget,
>   yet I will not forget you
>
> (Isa. 49:13–15)

Responding to the laments of the exilic community who deeply feels that God has abandoned them, God becomes the ultimate Mother who shows compassion. Even though earthly mothers, when under extreme duress, might forget their children (see the horrific images in Lam. 2:20; 4:10, where desperate mothers eat their own children), God as Mother will always be faithful. Once again this female metaphor for God is used in close proximity to a traditional male metaphor: God as Zion's Husband.[9]

Isaiah 66:10–13, a text that builds on Deutero-Isaiah, employs female imagery for the Divine in the context of the new challenges that face the people back home. The metaphor of the nurturing mother is used once more to depict God's restoration of Israel:

> Rejoice with Jerusalem, and be glad for her,
>   all you who love her;
> rejoice with her in joy,
>   all you who mourn over her—
> that you may nurse and be satisfied
>   from her consoling breast;
> that you may drink deeply with delight
>   from her glorious bosom.
>
> For thus says the LORD:
> I will extend prosperity to her like a river,
>   and the wealth of the nations like an overflowing stream;
> and you shall nurse and be carried on her arm,

> and dandled on her knees.
> As a mother comforts her child,
>   so I will comfort you;
>   you shall be comforted in Jerusalem
>   (Isa. 66:10–13)

After describing the rebirth of the people in terms of Mother Zion bringing forth the restored nation with the assistance of God as Midwife (Isa. 66:7–10), the prophet portrays God in verses 11–13 as Mother who comforts her children, who nurses and takes care of the newborn Israel. Scholars have offered a variety of suggestions as to why these remarkable female metaphors for God were created at that particular time. Mayer Gruber argues that Deutero-Isaiah, who reacts strongly against idolatry, may have used both masculine and feminine metaphors for God to counter the goddesses of other religions.[10] In response to Gruber, John Schmitt maintains that the female imagery for God relates to the frequent occurrence of Zion as a mother in Isaiah 40–66. Schmitt argues: "the motherhood of God parallels the motherhood of Zion in its goodness, its constancy, and its exuberant prodigality."[11] According to Rainer Albertz, after the exile people were disillusioned by the failure of lofty royal theology and slowly started once more to discern God's involvement in their everyday lives, in the domestic sphere.[12] It was in the birth of their children, recovery from illness, rain after a prolonged drought, and the bounty of the harvest that the exiles recognized God's presence and care. God's involvement in the micro-stories of their personal lives offered a paradigm for understanding the macro-story of their nation's future. In light of this development, it is fitting that in Deutero-Isaiah the hope for the future is captured in the familiar yet miraculous action of giving birth to a child.[13]

Whatever the origin of these striking metaphors, I propose that the female imagery used for God in these texts from Deutero- and Trito-Isaiah in conjunction with God's liberative and creative work fulfills a powerful rhetorical function in the overall theological argument of the book of Isaiah. Even though the female images for the Divine are few in number, they exhibit a transformation in the development of Israel's theological formulations and give rise to new understandings of God as Deliverer. It is precisely the balance between creativity and tradition that is at work in Israel's theological formulations that would help Israel to maintain and reclaim their religious identity and to survive the trauma of being carried off into exile. Moreover, it will be evident that these maternal metaphors—with their emphasis on new life, nurture, and care—offer rich resources for people recovering from trauma.

FACING THE EMPIRE

Joseph Blenkinsopp argues that Isaiah 40–48 may be read as a type of "propagandistic manifesto" to promote the reign of the Persian emperor Cyrus, who uprooted Israel's conqueror, the once mighty Babylonian Empire.[14] Deutero-Isaiah depicts God as the true Liberator, who chose Cyrus and led him to subjugate the Babylonians. Endowed with royal titles such as "God's shepherd" (Isa. 45:1) and "God's anointed" (Isa. 44:28), Cyrus is entrusted with the mission of bringing the exiles home and of restoring their religious cult. The prophet engages in various rhetorical strategies to convince his audience that this unexpected "political star" is indeed God's chosen one: the messiah.

This emphasis on Cyrus's role in God's plan for the restoration of Israel has led some scholars to argue that the first "servant song" (Isa. 42:1–4, together with its sequel in vv. 5–9) refers to Cyrus.[15] In this first song, God commissions a servant, filled with God's Spirit, to restore justice and freedom in debilitating circumstances, but without the customary violence and bloodshed associated with a battle for liberation. This interpretation may relate to Cyrus's commitment to reverse the harsh policies of his predecessors by sending home the exiled and by restoring the cults of the dispersed communities (Isa. 44:26–28).[16]

However, we should be careful not to romanticize this Persian emperor. Cyrus was not exempt from the violence associated with empires. In Deutero-Isaiah we see glimpses of this violence in the depiction of the fall of Babylon (Isa. 45:1–2; see also 47:1–3). It is further noteworthy that the violence is divinely ordained. In light of Deutero-Isaiah's tendency to portray the nations as instruments in the hands of the sovereign God, it is thus *God* who levels the mountains, breaks the bronze doors into pieces, cuts through iron bars, subdues nations, and strips kings of their royal cloaks.

The merging of God's power and sovereignty with what is happening in the geopolitical sphere is a strategy that any leader with visions of grandeur or dreams of "saving" the world would want to employ. It is thus important to consider why the Deutero-Isaianic prophet would seek to propagate imperial rule through his visions of the Divine. Edward Said writes how an important aspect of exiles' recovery is to "reconstitute their broken lives, usually by choosing to see themselves as part of a triumphant ideology or restored people."[17] One could imagine Deutero-Isaiah telling the story in such a way that the returning community would experience a new sense of a God-given purpose. The Israelites would have expected a redeemer from the Davidic line who would come to restore the house of Israel (e.g., Isa. 9:6–7; 11:1–10); however, Deutero-Isaiah seeks to turn the exiles' hopes toward an unlikely source of God's salvation: the Persian emperor. Deutero-Isaiah attempts to explain why it is Cyrus, and not a son of David, who has become the means by which the Creator-Redeemer God will bring salvation to God's people. Within this framework, the emphasis on the sovereign God who uses empires to execute God's will becomes somewhat more understandable. However, the rose-colored view of Cyrus as messiah did not last. Much as politicians today fall out of favor because they fail to deliver on election promises, the fact that there is no further mention of Cyrus in Isaiah 49–55 indicates disillusionment with his rule. Even though he was responsible for the return of the Jews and other exiles, the exiles were disappointed that the Davidic dynasty was not eventually restored. What's more, it soon became evident that the returning community in Judah would continue to suffer under new intrusive imperial politics—that of the Persian Empire.[18]

In light of this reality, the exilic community seems to have looked elsewhere for inspiration. In the remainder of Deutero-Isaiah there is a much greater emphasis on the city of Zion (Jerusalem) as the locus of hope. The focus has turned from the greater political arena back to the community, broken and despised, who is urged to serve as God's instruments in the world, effecting God's salvation.[19] In this regard, Walter Brueggemann argues that there were Israelites who sided with the empire, but that "the ones who mattered in the long run were those who kept their critical distance, who regularly reminded the empire of that which it wanted to forget: that human power is penultimate, that there are limits to the power of the empire, and that the power finally is judged according to its enactments of mercy, compassion, and justice."[20] In the midst of the dominant story line, written in support of the empire, one finds a few anti-imperial strands rooted in compassion, mercy, and love; these strands offer a glimpse of an alternative way of resisting the empire. In Isaiah 47:6, for example, we read how God has revoked Babylon's power because they failed to show mercy: "On the aged you made your yoke exceedingly heavy." Brueggemann argues that the empire should have been merciful—particularly to those who were at their most vulnerable.

This emphasis on mercy and compassion as a means to resist the power of the empire is also evident in the number of female metaphors that are used in Deutero-Isaiah to portray the Divine.[21] It is significant that in Isaiah 40–48 we also find two occurrences of God as Mother in Labor, which evokes a vision of an alternative world rooted in life and love (Isa. 42:14; 45:10). And in Isaiah 49 the shift in focus from the broader political sphere to the city and her inhabitants is accompanied by the compelling metaphor of God as Nurturing Mother. It seems that this compassionate female metaphor plays a key role in communicating a different way of being in the world (Isa. 49:14–15).

RHETORICAL SIGNIFICANCE OF THE FEMALE IMAGERY FOR THE DIVINE IN DEUTERO-ISAIAH

God as Mother in Labor: A New Beginning

The metaphor in Isaiah 42 and 45 of God as Mother in Labor plays an important role in denoting the sense of a new beginning that is vital for the exiles who have been subjected to large-scale upheaval and disorientation. Edward Said remarks that exile is very much like "death without death's ultimate mercy," tearing "millions of people from the nourishment of tradition, family, and geography."[22] For the survivors of the Babylonian exile, the experience of losing their land, temple, families, and homes was like dying. Deutero-Isaiah introduces themes of new life associated with the metaphor of a mother in labor to point toward the restoration of God's people: the birth of a nation. This notion of rebirth is often present in the way trauma survivors express their experiences of recovery. Flora Keshgegian notes that survivors of the Armenian genocide talk in almost triumphant terms of being reborn. For trauma survivors throughout the ages, to live through the trauma and to start a new life seems to be the most successful means of recovering—the ultimate revenge.[23]

As the Israelites were pondering God's ability or willingness to act on their behalf, the prophet introduced a familiar metaphor, namely that of a Raging Warrior. But then he juxtaposed it with a new metaphor: a woman crying out in pain, gasping and panting on the verge of giving birth. The woman in childbirth served as a dramatic reminder that a change was about to occur. Instead of death, associated with the warrior's actions (v. 13), the metaphor of a mother in labor (v. 14) introduced the promise of new life that God would create for the exiles by delivering them from captivity.

The metaphor of God as Mother in Labor offers a creative means of merging creation and deliverance themes. The gasps and panting of a mother in labor offer a new interpretation of the creation imagery in Isaiah 42 (see v. 5) and the surrounding verses (see Isa. 40:12, 28; 41:17–20; 43:1, 7) and serve as a powerful image of deliverance.[24] This metaphor is even more powerful if we consider that, in antiquity, childbirth quite often entailed the death of the mother or the baby or both, and that a successful birth was celebrated as an act of deliverance in praise songs that depicted the mother in labor as a war hero who had won the battle for liberation. The mother risked death and was the deliverer of new life just as the warrior risked death and was the deliverer of autonomy and peace for the nation.[25]

This commitment to life that underlies God's acts of deliverance is seen in the radical transformation enacted by God in Isaiah 42:15, which follows directly after the metaphor of God as Mother in Labor in verse 14. In a dramatic cosmic upheaval, God levels the mountains and hills and turns the rivers and pools into dry land. This reversal continues a central theme in Isaiah 40, in which the language of valleys being filled up and hills being brought low (vv. 3–4) signals God's resolve to lead the exiles back home. The language of turning darkness into light and of leveling rough places indicates God's determination to remove all obstacles before the returnees.[26] In Isaiah 42:16 this intent is made explicit when God leads the blind, guiding them safely on unknown paths. God's deliverance is thus very much imaged as both clearing away and building up; destroying impediments (like a warrior) as well as ensuring new life (like a mother).

In the second occurrence of God as Mother in Labor, in Isaiah 45, the theme of new life that underlies God's deliverance continues in a different fashion. In order to show God's resolve to do something new, the metaphor of God as Mother in Labor is employed in conjunction with the metaphors of God as Potter and God as Father. As noted earlier, the point of comparison between these interanimating metaphors is their ability to create something new. The metaphors of a mother in labor, a father that sires a child, and a potter that molds clay offer unique perspectives on the traditional understanding of God as Creator of heaven and earth (Isa. 45:7–8). Drawing on an Ancient Near-Eastern custom that the idol makers' creations are not alive until they are born, Sarah Dille argues that the mother and father imagery, together with the potter metaphor, indicates that this new creation is given life by God's self.[27]

One should note that, despite the promise of new life and the hope of deliverance, the metaphor of a mother in labor does not negate the reality of pain experienced by the trauma victims. Thus, in Isaiah 42, the cries and panting of a woman overcome by labor pains quite vividly remind the reader that a key aspect of giving birth is excruciating pain. Employing this metaphor for God may suggest that God is entering into the victim's pain, sharing the trials of people who have been deeply traumatized by being forcefully removed from their homes, taken to a foreign land, and living as exiles far away from all that was familiar. This metaphor strongly suggests that God is not a far-removed, uncaring deity. On the contrary, the prophet assures the people of God's presence and concern. Like a mother working hard to bring a baby into the world, God is identifying with the people's pain.

Therefore, the metaphor of God as Mother in Labor conveys a profound mixture of suffering and pain, hope and joy. Introducing this metaphor in a context of liberation points to the fact that God does experience the people's pain but also moves beyond the pain in order to make new life possible for the exilic returnees.

God as Nurturing Mother: Preserving Life

The second maternal metaphor used for God—God as Nurturing Mother, in Isaiah 49 and 66—continues the emphasis on new life, but with an added focus on God's love, which is associated with the compassion of mothers. The exiles faced a profound existential and theological crisis and were in desperate need of compassion and care. The female metaphor of a mother's nurturing love that is used for God spoke to the crushed and tormented exiles as they were recovering from the trauma they had experienced in a way few other metaphors could. The maternal metaphor for God assured the exiles of God's genuine love for God's children, maintaining that it was God's compassionate love that was responsible for the new life that God would create by letting the exiles return home (Isa. 49:9–10) and rebuild their city.

The agonizing cries of the daughter Zion in the book of Lamentations (1:12–16; 20–22) are echoed in Isaiah 49:14: "The LORD has forsaken me, my LORD has forgotten me." In stark contrast to God's earlier silence in the book of Lamentations, in Isaiah 49:15 God seeks to convince the people that God's love surpasses even the strongest bond between mothers and their children.[28] It is this deep love for God's children that will be responsible for Mother Zion's children returning to her, carried by queens and kings who will act as their surrogate mothers and nursemaids (Isa. 49:18–23). Zion will be surprised to see the sheer abundance of children returning—her tent will be too small for all the future inhabitants of the city.

Isaiah describes a dramatic reversal of the judgment formerly pronounced by the prophet Jeremiah: Instead of experiencing humiliation at the hands of her former captors, Zion will be glorified—the nations will pay homage to her. Though she has been threatened with divorce in Jeremiah 2–3, in Deutero-Isaiah she will be reconciled with God (Isa. 54:5–8). In the book of Lamentations, Zion is portrayed as sitting all alone, mourning her own condition as well as the loss of her children (Lam. 1:1–3); in Deutero-Isaiah, there will be an abundance of life in her midst as her children return from afar.[29]

The metaphor of a nurturing mother conveys the notion that it is not enough that God gives new life; it also suggests that, in order for new life to continue, it needs to be nurtured and preserved. In Deutero-Isaiah, a central aspect of this understanding of a mother's ongoing task of comforting and caring is the theme of provision and protection. Evoking the ancient traditions of God's provision of water in the wilderness (Exod. 15:22–25; 17:1–7; Num. 20:2–13; Deut. 8:15), Deutero-Isaiah describes God's nurturing love in terms of God causing springs of water to gush up and creating rivers in the desert (Isa. 43:20; also 35:7). And in Isaiah 49:9–10, this theme is continued when God provides the liberated exiles with food and drink on their journey through the wilderness. In contrast to their journey into exile many years ago, the returnees will not hunger or thirst, nor will the brutal elements—the scorching sun and wind—torment them. Evoking associations of God as Shepherd, which was featured in Isaiah 40:11, God leads the returning exiles to pastures and springs in the most inhospitable of terrains.

The metaphor of a nurturing mother is also at work in Isaiah 66:7–13.[30] In light of the ongoing economic, social, and political challenges that faced the exiles after they returned home, Israel continued to be in need of the compassion and care offered by the metaphor of God as Mother. Imaginatively merging the metaphors of a Mother in Labor (now applied to Zion) and a Nurturing Mother (both Zion and God), Isaiah 66 describes Judah's restoration by employing female imagery. Zion's labor pains will be brief, indicating that God, acting as Midwife (see also chapter 4), will not delay bringing new life into the world (vv. 7–8).

Isaiah 66 expands this connection between new life and the need that it be preserved by means of ongoing care offered to the newborn baby tended by its two mothers: Zion and God.[31] Accordingly, an image of nursing is used to depict God's provision of food and drink that will ensure that the newborn not only survives but also thrives. The inhabitants of Jerusalem will "nurse and be satisfied from her [Zion's] consoling breast," and the community of exilic survivors will "drink deeply with delight from her glorious bosom" (v. 11). God will "extend prosperity to her like a river, and the wealth of the nations like an overflowing stream" (v. 12). This reversal of fortunes that will secure the well-being of Judah is once more depicted in terms of a baby being nursed and cradled by its mother(s): "You shall nurse and be carried on her arm, and dandled on her knees" (see also v. 13, where God is likened to a mother comforting her child).

In the midst of these touching descriptions of the metaphor of God's nurturing love, we once more pick up references to the deep-seated memory of the trauma lurking below the surface. In Isaiah 49, the reference to God as the ideal mother who will never forget or abandon her children evokes the pain of mothers who actually have forgotten or abandoned their children—as so often happens in a situation of war where parents and children become separated.[32] The female metaphors that are used for God in these Deutero-Isaianic texts offer a means of acknowledging these horrors and pain before moving on, and so allowing this important phase in the grieving process. The confession that God is the Mother whose love knows no bounds serves the function of naming the pain and rebuilding the bond between God and God's traumatized children who have suffered from the fear of being forsaken by God. It is by remembering the horror of mothers abandoning their children and then invoking the metaphor of God as Nurturing Mother, that the pain of abandoning and being abandoned is confronted.

Recoding Power

In chapter 1 of this book, I mentioned that one of the potential problems with the metaphor of God as Liberator-Warrior is the way in which this divine metaphor has been used and abused by those in power. As noted before, the theme of God's power or sovereignty was indeed very important in an exilic context, where people harbored serious questions about God's ability to intervene and effect change. As an image of restoration, God's sovereignty served as a prophetic response to the questions regarding God's apparent powerlessness and absence. The Deutero-Isaianic prophet strongly asserts that God is able to act decisively in people's lives to undo the powers that sought the destruction of Israel and to return the exiles home. It is this emphasis on God's sovereignty that explains the prophet's tendency to use powerful metaphors like God as Mighty Warrior (Isa. 42:13), God as Influential Redeemer (Isa. 44:6), and God as Potter who has the power to shape his creations any way he pleases (Isa. 45:9).

Understanding what the prophet was doing in his own time and context is only a first step. One of the underlying assumptions of this book is that, as responsible biblical interpreters, we have to ask critical questions about the way these metaphors function within contemporary contexts. In this regard, Catherine Keller warns against the danger in contemporary America's tendency to uncritically apply language and imagery that denote an all-powerful God: "A theology of omnipotence electrifies the halo of American domination. Where then does the idolatry lie—in the fact that the United States plays God, or . . . that it imitates a false God? Does the idolatry lie in our emulation of a divine superpower or in our confusion of God with omnipotence in the first place? A theopolitics of omnipotence is clearly at work in imperialism. But is there imperialism within the doctrine of omnipotence?"[33]

Keller has identified a key problem in using biblical texts in modern political discourse. The fact of the matter is that Deutero-Isaiah does advocate an image of a sovereign God, a God whose power is without measure (Isa. 40:12). However, as Keller further suggests, a vital aspect in countering an imperial mind-set would be to start decoding divine power. The same rhetoric that gave hope to a battle-weary community in the context of Isaiah sounds quite different when a superpower, like the United States, uses this religious rhetoric to afford divine sanction to its foreign policy.[34]

A good example of decoding divine power comes from Rita Nakashima Brock, who comments on the rhetorical effect of introducing female imagery in a military and/or patriarchal context in order to present the reader with an alternative understanding of power. Using the intriguing image in Jeremiah 31:22, which describes the new thing that God is about to create in terms of a future where "a female shall surround the warrior," Brock argues: "At every point in the text [Jeremiah 31], a female with divine connections surrounds the powers that threaten to destroy life, surrounds not by defeat or conquest, but by loving compassion. Surrounding suggests a new form of power, the power of grief and repentance, of the overcoming of pain and suffering, of neutralizing violence and death, and of transforming defiance and shame through the embracing of—the risking of encounter with—that which threatens and frightens us in our very midst."[35] Brock argues that Jeremiah 31 reflects disenchantment with traditional power structures. As a result, the prophet is looking for an alternative means of expressing the traditional understanding of God's power and finds this alternative in what Brock calls "maternal thinking"—a paradigm of hope that is "grounded in the new presence of strategies and values already present in the people hidden in the dominated lives of women."[36] Thus, instead of the masculine power represented by the centralized government that the prophet deems responsible for Israel's fall, Jeremiah 31 focuses on the power of motherly love and compassion—equally strong but offering a markedly different way of thinking about power.

I argue that a similar dynamic is at work in Deutero-Isaiah's application of female metaphors for the Divine. We can make fruitful use of the female metaphors (such as God as Mother in Labor and God as Nurturing Mother) that are used in the midst of the prophet's proclamation of a sovereign God, to decode and subsequently recode the power of God. According to Catherine Keller, the alternative to divine omnipotence is not impotence. In contrast to divine power that draws its associations from military force or from the political or social influence of the patriarch, I suggest that we recode God's power in terms of the power that emerges from love. The female metaphors in Deutero-Isaiah are particularly well-suited to encourage us to think differently about God's power, because they serve as a reminder of alternative values, of a mother's power to first give life and then nurture that life.

The fact that the metaphor of God as Liberator-Warrior is juxtaposed with the metaphor of a mother in labor, who is about to bring life into this world (Isa. 42:13–14), challenges us to regard the traditional, military-orientated metaphor of God in new ways.[37]

These metaphors impact on one another. The Liberator-Warrior metaphor is altered markedly by the presence of the female metaphor. Together they bestow fresh meaning on the traditional metaphor of God as Deliverer; in particular, they help us to think differently about God's power. The metaphor of God as Mother in Labor evokes the power of new life that counters or subverts the power to take life away.

This is a creative power, shared by every other woman who had ever given birth or who would ever give birth. Also in Isaiah 45, within the context of graphic violence perpetrated by a destructive deity breaking down an empire, the metaphor of a mother giving birth is suggestive of another reality: new life that needs to be nurtured.

However, the warrior imagery also transforms the metaphor of a woman giving birth. As noted before, the metaphor of God as Mother in Labor captures something of the fragile nature of Israel's experience—the life-and-death situation in which they found themselves and which is amplified by its juxtaposition with the warrior metaphor. We should not forget that childbearing was a treacherous affair in those times; women all too often died in labor, just as warriors died in battle. Using these provocative metaphors for God contributes to an understanding of the vulnerability of the people who dared to depict the vulnerability of God. However, even though both the mother and the warrior are in danger and hence quite vulnerable, both are exceedingly strong. The cries and panting of a woman in labor is not a sign of weakness but of strength; a sign of her determination to ensure that her child enters the world alive and healthy. Similarly, God's willingness to enter into the people's suffering, which is evidence of God's great love, is coupled with God's resolve to act by bringing forth new life. Thus, the metaphor of God as Mother in Labor offers an extraordinary mixture of active power in the midst of vulnerability; that is, of a God who is as vulnerable and at the same time as powerful as a woman giving birth.

We find another opportunity to decode God's power in the introduction of the female metaphor of God as Nurturing Mother in Isaiah 49:13–14. Significantly, in previous prophetic books the relationship between God and Zion has been described in terms of a male deity and the nation or city as his wife. According to the books of Hosea, Jeremiah, Ezekiel, and Lamentations, which portray the events leading up to the destruction of Zion in terms of domestic violence, the history of the courtship and married life of God and Zion is not a happy one (see Jer. 2–3; Ezek. 16, 21; Hos. 1–2; Lam. 1). The "wife" is beaten, stripped, and cast out; moreover, the text depicts her punishment as something she brought on herself by being disobedient—a classic justification for such violence.[38]

The breakdown in relationship, the punishment of the wife for her unfaithfulness, the brutal violence of tearing down the walls of the city and defiling her sanctuaries all presume actions of sheer power on the part of a male deity. In light of this portrayal, the repeated references to

God's comfort imagined in terms of a mother's love seem to be misplaced. As the ruling metaphor of a Divine Liberator-Warrior was interrupted by God as Mother in Labor (Isa. 42:13–14), so the metaphor of an abusive husband is interrupted by God as Nurturing Mother (Isa. 49:13–15). Once again, it is significant that the presence of this female metaphor—which is rooted in love and compassion—changes, alters, or balances the typical understanding of violent male power that in previous instances describes God's relationship to the people. The divine metaphor of God as Powerful Patriarch who holds the fate of his wife (and children and subordinates) in his hand is transformed by the compassionate love of a mother who will do anything to keep her children healthy and safe. That said, we should not romanticize a mother's love or assume that women are exempted from engaging in violence. There are numerous examples of women who were prepared to resort to violence to protect themselves or, especially, their children.

In the following section, I shall show how this power that is rooted in compassion is presented as possessing the remarkable ability to effect change in ways that is responsible for human flourishing. The female imagery in Deutero-Isaiah contributes to the creation of an alternative servant-community where the new life that God is creating by means of God's compassionate love is not confined to the exiles alone.

Compassion's Power

It is significant that, in two of the instances where female metaphors are used in Deutero-Isaiah, we also encounter the enigmatic figure of the servant of God (Isa. 42:1–7 and 49:1–6).[39] The vocation and identity of the servant of God in these texts show a remarkable correspondence with the connotations conveyed by the female imagery that has been used to describe the deliverance by God.

In Isaiah 42:1–7, the servant—God's chosen one, who enjoys God's special favor (v. 1)—is called to bring forth justice (vv. 1, 4), to be a light to the nations (v. 6), to open the eyes of those who are blind, and to release those who are trapped in prisons of darkness (v. 7). As in the metaphor of the Mother in Labor, one finds here an example of profound power in the midst of vulnerability in the person of the servant of God, who has become known as the "suffering servant." In verse 3, the servant is described as "a bruised reed" and "a dimly burning wick." However, because of God's Spirit that works through him, the servant will not be broken or quenched; instead, he will faithfully continue his mission. This portrayal of power in the midst of powerlessness is continued in Isaiah 49:1–6. Even though the servant feels that his efforts are in vain (v. 4), his seeming failure is supplanted by God's power, which serves as the source of the servant's strength (v. 5). By bringing about the return of the exiles, God will extend the servant's reach beyond the narrow confines of Israel to serve as a light to all the nations, so that God's salvation may extend to the ends of the earth (v. 6).

The servant of God imagery, which is closely aligned with the female metaphors of God as Mother in Labor and as Nurturing Mother, challenges us to think differently about power. The power of the mother's love stands over and against the traditional understanding of violence and bloodshed associated with the warrior. This alternative understanding of power could conceivably be explained with reference to the precarious situation in which the exilic community found itself. In Jeremiah 31:8, the text that Brock uses to argue in favor of an alternative form of power, we find the following provocative statement about God's resolve to return the exiles home:

> See, I am going to bring them from the land of the north,
> and gather them from the farthest parts of the earth,
> among them the blind and the lame,
> those with child and those in labor, together;
> a great company, they shall return here.
>
> (Jer. 31:8)

As Kathleen O'Connor points out, in this text the exiles are identified "as the weak, the wounded, and the vulnerable"—those with physical ailments or people who hold little political or social power. The strange truth about this text is that this group of vulnerable people with little power may be able to make a difference by embracing an alternative kind of power, another way of being in the world: one that reaches out to others in compassion rather than in self-defensive violence. As O'Conner describes this alternative reality held up in Jeremiah 31:8, "But they have the critical and astonishing power to give birth and to make a future people for those who thought they were doomed. How can the blind and the vulnerable lead? How can those giving birth march? Both groups—not kings, queens, or warriors, but wounded survivors—are the new community, limping homeward. Broken yet fertile, they carry the future."[40]

The theme of extending God's comfort and love to others

encourages us to think more broadly about the very nature of mothering. Sarah Ruddick argues that a mother's actions could well be extended to include other children besides her own. For Ruddick, mothering is not contingent on giving birth. She argues that stepmothers or adoptive mothers, or fathers for that matter, are no less qualified to undertake maternal tasks for not having given birth. This broader understanding of mothering implies "a commitment to protect the lives of 'other' children, to resist on behalf of children assaults on body or spirit that violate the promise of birth."[41]

A mother's power is rooted in compassion; it flows from being concerned about the needs and interests of the other. It will be the power of compassion, particularly personified in the figure of the Mother God's devotion and love (which stands in contrast to the efforts of fallible human mothers), that not only brings forth new life but also works diligently to preserve life. It will also be this compassion that will be the driving force behind the servant's vocation to be the light of and to bring justice to the nations—a mission not executed by force, but in a gentle, noncoercive way.

With this in mind, Ann Johnston argues that "this rebirth of Israel is not for the sake of Israel alone and her continued existence." Citing the servant language in Isaiah 49:6, Johnston points out that Israel is, instead, called to be a servant community; to be salvific by means of compassion and suffering in the lives of others far beyond the narrow confines of Judah and Jerusalem.[42] The nurturing maternal imagery in Isaiah 49 thus reminds the exiles that, just as they are themselves in need of comfort and care, so they, in the midst of their suffering, are still called to remember those who find themselves in even greater need.

The metaphor of the compassionate God who "mothers" the bereaved exiles and who calls God's children to "mother" others offers a means to resist the imperial powers that ultimately fail to sustain new life. What could be called a maternal or parental ethic, with its emphasis on nurture of and care for the newborn Israel, serves as reminder of the very possibility of an alternative world. The nurturing metaphors in Deutero-Isaiah denote a different kind of power of an individual or a group of people who, in the midst of brokenness, in spite of brokenness, and maybe even because of the brokenness, is called not to destroy the nations but to be the bearer of light and justice to the other.

Acting without Seeing the End

The very presence of these female metaphors for God that are so different from the traditional warrior image contributes to a sense of God's incomprehensibility. Significantly, in all four instances where female metaphors are used for God, they occur in conjunction with some other well-known male metaphors. The merger of these seemingly disjunctive metaphors serves as an important rhetorical strategy to challenge the exiles to look differently at God. Patricia Tull Willey notes that the paradoxical nature of this imagery makes it impossible for the reader to take these metaphors literally. The juxtaposition of God as Liberator-Warrior/Mother in Labor (Isa. 42), God as Mother/Father/Potter (Isa. 45), God as both Husband and Mother (Isa. 49), and God as Mother/Midwife (Isa. 66) help us to understand that God is more complex than the human roles we imagine.

This refusal to capture God in a single metaphor agrees with Deutero-Isaiah's fierce anti-idol polemic; the "my-God-is-bigger-than-your-God theology" that forms a central theme in Isaiah 44 as well as Deutero-Isaiah as a whole (see also Isa. 40:18–20). It is vital for the prophet to assert that God is the sovereign God; the Creator and Deliverer God who cannot be captured in wood or stone or in any such form. The paradoxical formulation in Isaiah 45:7—with its assertion that God creates both light and darkness, prosperity and peace (shalom) as well as disaster (evil)—conveys the belief that God cannot be defined in words or captured in concrete imagery. This claim is underscored by the enigmatic formulation in verse 15 that God is a God who hides God's self. The hiddenness of God belongs to God's freedom and refusal to be contained by or known in terms of conventional categories.[43] In a world where theological thinking is often fraught with simplicity and easy answers, the female imagery that is used for God may offer the opportunity to image God with a greater sense of complexity, thus avoiding the dangers of oversimplification.

The interanimation of metaphors in the Deutero-Isaianic texts, in which the female metaphors play a vital role, has a second important function: The disjunctive nature of the metaphors may encourage believers to regard the complexity of their own situation in a new way. The emphasis on complexity and ambiguity in the divine imagery reflects the complexity of the geopolitical situation in which Israel found itself. This complexity is, for example, evident in the paradox mentioned in Isaiah 40–48: that God was using Cyrus, a heathen emperor who did not know God (Isa. 45:4–5), to bring about the deliverance of God's people. For Deutero-Isaiah it was important to show that God was very much involved with the geopolitical reality of the day, using empires to punish the wayward Israel (see Isa. 5:26–30; 10:5–6) and subsequently also to build a future for God's people. However, Cyrus did not live up to the prophet's hopes, or the political reality did not quite work out the way that the prophet had hoped for. And, as we learn from subsequent texts, the process of restoration was much messier than the prophet had imagined initially.

The complexity of imagery used for God also resonates with the presentation of Israel's oppressors in Isaiah 49. Immediately following a beautiful depiction of God's compassionate love (49:13–15) we find a very human response to trauma, a terrifying description of Israel's fantasies of revenge and the humiliation of their former oppressors: their captors consuming their own flesh, intoxicated by their own blood (49:26), and prostrating themselves in front of Zion (49:23).[44] These violent images are offset against the nurturing images of God that articulate hope for the future despite the ambiguities and messiness of the present situation.

The Mother in Labor metaphor moreover illustrates that God's work proceeds in secret: the infant's presence may become noticeable, but the child remains unseen by the human eye until it is born. The secret nature of gestation makes the powerful point that God is at work even though it may not always be evident to the observer. The pregnancy metaphor, the length of time when not much seems to be happening, may well explain why God seemed to be inactive for so long. At the same time, it powerfully asserts that God will bring new life into the world as well as provide the comfort and care necessary to sustain this new life.

The female metaphors for God offer quite an intriguing means to describe something of the ambiguity and uncertainty present in the theological assertion that God is creating a future for Israel. The metaphors of a mother in labor and a nurturing mother capture the hope and possibilities for new life, but they also communicate the uncertainty of not knowing exactly how this child will turn out or whether the child will even survive infancy. Sarah Ruddick explains the precariousness that accompanies the act of mothering: "To give birth is to create a life that cannot be kept safe, whose unfolding cannot be controlled and whose eventual death is certain. . . . In a world beyond one's control, to be humble is to have a profound sense of the limits of one's actions and of the unpredictability of the consequences of one's work."[45] The unwavering commitment to act in a way that will ensure the preservation of this fragile existence has compelled mothers—and fathers—throughout the ages to continue to mother despite unexpected setbacks and hardships. Even the happiest children are at times ill, lonely, selfish, angry, temperamental, mean-spirited, or afraid.[46] The prophet likens God's action to these human actions of occasional disciplining, but also nurturing, providing, and educating that occur moment-by-moment, day-by-day, in hope but without certainty of what the outcome will be.

A TURN TO LOVE

At the beginning of this chapter, I mentioned that the book of Deutero-Isaiah constituted survival literature that had originated from a situation where people were experiencing a profound sense of powerlessness generated by the trauma caused by the exile. A typical human reaction to such trauma is to lash out in anger and revenge, to humiliate one's enemies. Deutero-Isaiah offers an alternative response, namely that Israel was called to live by compassion and not by coercion. As Paul Hanson argues, "Following the example of the God who entered into solidarity with the powerless, humans enter into the task of constructing a society and world in which mutuality and cooperation become habits of the heart and justice and liberty the marks of human society."[47]

As I have shown in this chapter, the female imagery that is used in conjunction with the deliverance by God in Deutero-Isaiah contributes to the creation of a counter reality that offers a means of resisting the empire while being in the midst of it. The metaphors of God as Mother in Labor and as Mother who Nurtures her newborn subvert the violence presumed and affected by the empire. These metaphors do so by drawing the readers' attention to life and to love, by inspiring them to act in ways that nurture and preserve life. This attention to life and love appears in the work of theologian Catherine Keller, who proposes a "counter-imperial ecology of love"[48] that builds on the work of postcolonial scholar Gayatri Spivak who proposes that change for the benefit of the whole world can occur only "through the supplementation of collective effort by love."[49] Spivak describes this love as the slow, attentive, mutual, collective effort to change policies and minds regarding laws, economics, education, and health care.[50] Welcoming the initiative of postcolonial theorists such as that of Spivak, Keller explores the possibility of "a theopolitics of planetary love" for those who "are in but not of the empire," who are called "to come out of the empire." This incentive to offer an alternative to empire is based on a love that cannot be disembodied; a love that is a "collective effort" that arises "across and between boundaries—of nations, faiths, groups, genders"; a love that understands that "all bodies matter." But, as Keller rightly points out, such a "vision requires an almost inhuman surplus of care."[51] Such an alternative vision that is rooted in, but not limited to, a parent's love and commitment to life can surely speak to the challenges arising out of the geopolitical scene. It is a love that, as Keller argues, "desires our fullest becoming—our genesis—as individuals, peoples, religions, nations."[52]

Considering the complex geopolitical context of the modern world, this turn to love may sound like madness. Hanson describes similar rejection in the fourth servant song (Isa. 52:13–53:12), which suggests the suffering and disappointment that the prophet experienced when his vision of a different world was not generally accepted.[53] It is further evident from the way in which Isaiah 49 ends, namely with an exuberant exhortation of the Liberator-Warrior God of Israel who engages in violence (vv. 25–26), that the story line of violence became the dominant one in Isaiah's time, as it is today.

However, as I argued in chapter 1, the very presence of minor voices can transform the dominant metaphor. The images of nurturing and new life introduced by the female imagery, though muted, tend to linger. The ambiguities of the text continue to confront us, and they await the future reader. As Robert Gibbs writes, "to knit diverse things together is the responsibility of holding open the meaning for a reader yet to come."[54] It may be that the times we are facing impress on us the urgency of picking up on these muted voices in the biblical text, thus finding language for God that contributes to the creation of an alternative moral imagination, rooted in love and compassion.

Continuing in this task, we now turn to the third image that contributes to an alternative understanding of God as Deliverer: God as Midwife, a metaphor that serves as a powerful expression of active power in the midst of distress.

Chapter 4

God as Midwife

MIDWIVES

This project on finding different ways of speaking about God's deliverance really started with the striking metaphor of God as Midwife. This metaphor is used in two psalms to describe God's acts of deliverance:

> Yet it was you who took me from the womb;
>> you kept me safe on my mother's breast.
> On you I was cast from my birth,
>> and since my mother bore me you have been my God.
>> (Ps. 22:9–10)

> Upon you I have leaned from my birth;
>> it was you who took me from my mother's womb.
>> (Ps. 71:6)

In a society where most babies are born in hospitals surrounded by well-trained doctors, gynecologists, pediatricians, nurses, and anesthetists, we may be unaware of the significant role played by midwives in bringing new life into the world. However, not everyone around the world has trained medical professionals on hand to deliver their babies. Zimbabwean theologian Sophia Chirongoma states that, since 1990, twice as many women have died in childbirth in the Zimbabwean capital's hospitals—one being her cousin, Christine.[1]

This reality helps us to appreciate the role of midwives in ancient society better. With strong hearts and gentle hands, midwives throughout the ages have helped women give birth. Today still, knowledge about childbirth passed down from mother to daughter plays a pivotal role in helping to prevent the deaths of both mothers and babies.[2] The fact that a large percentage of women around the world have no access to medical care means that modern midwives continue to preserve life through skills and wisdom passed down from generation to generation.[3]

The metaphor of God as Midwife is not the conventional way of thinking of deliverance by God—this image occurs only in a very few instances in the biblical tradition (Pss. 22, 71 and Isa. 66:7–9). However, the powerful connotations carried by this metaphor offer intriguing possibilities for contemplating the liberating presence of God. This image denotes an intimate connection between God and God's people similar to that which exists between a mother in labor and the midwife. In her study on the relationship between gender and healing in the ancient world, Elaine Wainwright writes, "At the centre of this female space occupied by midwife and pregnant woman are the bodies of women. Bodies touch as the hands of the midwife enable the birth process in and from the body of the other woman."[4] Drawing on feminist philosopher Elizabeth Grosz, who writes that "the toucher is always touched," Wainwright considers the imaginative possibilities embedded in this "female space of childbirth," particularly with reference to the incredible power of touch.[5]

PRAYING FROM THE DEPTHS OF THE DEEP

Thus far I have given several examples of individuals and communities coming to terms with the effects of severe trauma. Few instances so vividly reflect the struggle of dealing with the long, dark night of despair than the psalms of lament. From "the depths of the earth" [těhōmōt hā 'āreṣ] in Psalm 71:20—a powerful symbol of the vulnerable situation in which the believer finds him-/herself; from the watery chaos of the deep, the anguished cries for help rise up to the Deliverer God. In Psalm 71:2, the psalmist evokes the memory of the Deliverer God whose righteous deeds and saving acts form the basis for her[6] repeated petitions for deliverance: "In your righteousness deliver me and rescue me; incline your ear to me and save me. . . ." And in Psalm 22:19–21, the believer's cry to the Deliverer God is powerfully voiced: "But you, O LORD, do not be far away! O my help, come quickly to my aid! Deliver my soul from the sword, my life from the power of the dog! Save me from the mouth of the lion! From the horns of the wild oxen you have rescued me."

These psalms express feelings of torment and pain so compellingly that they have continued to capture the experiences of people traumatized by personal and corporeal tragedies. Scholars have suggested that Psalms 71 and 22 may convey the prayers not only of individuals but also of the community as a whole. The first-person plural reading in Psalm 71:20 suggests that the community of faith read this psalm together. Marvin Tate proposes that the historical setting of Psalm 71 seems to fit the early postexilic period (similar to that of Deutero-Isaiah), when the Israelites struggled for survival under an oppressive empire.[7] Similarly, James Mays notes that it is generally accepted that an individual prayer such as Psalm 22 may serve as a paradigm for the whole community. Yet, this communal application of the psalms does not nullify the validity of the prayer for the individual speaker who identifies his/her own well-being with that of the nation.[8] Read communally, these psalms may indeed reflect the pain and suffering that individuals and the community as a whole experienced under the brutal yoke of the empire. Samuel Balentine argues that the postexilic community in Judah dealt with continuous threats to their daily existence under the Persian Empire. The latter's imperial policies and heavy taxation inhibited individual economic and social stability.[9]

Coming to terms with trauma is a long and arduous road. Karen Baker-Fletcher reminds us that, in contemporary conflicts around the world, "truth and reconciliation" or deliverance and healing is a process.[10] The effects of trauma may linger long after the initial event. Psalms (such as Psalm 71 and Psalm 22) that offer an intimate glimpse of how a believer or community deals with the ongoing effects of trauma provide readers with the opportunity to reflect on how they may cope after a devastating blow. Balentine suggests that psalms formed part of Israel's survival strategy: Israel was called to grieve hard for what was lost, ultimately finding a way through the impediments of a less-than-perfect life.[11]

Examining the impact of traumatic experiences—such as child abuse, genocide (including her own family's experience of Armenian genocide as well as those of Holocaust survivors), and the African American experience of slavery—feminist theologian Flora Keshgegian argues that, in order for victims of trauma to heal, they need to develop "a practice of remembering that is multiple, complex, and inclusive." This practice includes (1) the candid recollection of suffering and loss that is always threatened by forgetfulness and even erasure; (2) the memory of moments of resistance that arose during suffering and attest to the resilience and persistence of the human spirit; (3) the recollection of life experience and connections beyond the suffering that testify to life beyond trauma.[12]

Keshgegian asks in particular how victims of severe trauma recover to form a "new self." The formation of the "new self" includes goals such as "reclaiming a sustaining faith and reclaiming the world," "reconnecting with others and nurturing relationships," thus exhibiting "a renewed and fuller sense of commitment to life."[13] With these goals in mind, Keshgegian explores the role of memory as a process of healing and transformation; how memories of past suffering and memories of resistance may become redeeming memories.

In Psalm 71, we see how the psalmist, joining the laments of other believers who have been equally threatened, honestly confronts the memory of his own pain; he does not shy away from naming the threats that inhibit his life and cause him harm. In verses 9–12, the psalmist formulates the fear of being abandoned by God (see also the anguished cry of God-forsakenness in Ps. 22:1). However, the believer invokes the memory of God's past acts of deliverance. With confidence, the psalmist remembers God's involvement in his life when he speaks of God's support since his youth (vv. 5–6). By referring to God's "mighty" and "wondrous deeds" (vv. 15–17), he ecstatically recalls God's saving acts in Israel's history and alludes to God's presence and protection, as in the paradigmatic events at the Red Sea (Exod. 14–15). Memories of God's deeds of liberation encourage the psalmist to continue praying for deliverance and to resist his current tormented state by refusing to be a victim who resigns himself to abuse.

In Psalms 71 and 22 we find, moreover, evidence of surviving trauma, of moving on. In both psalms, the believer praises God for deliverance, suggesting a capacity for looking beyond current circumstances toward something new. Psalm 22 includes signs of reconnection, the ability to create a new self in relation to others. Together these psalms offer a remarkable glimpse of a long and winding journey through pain on the way to healing.

RUPTURING GOD-LANGUAGE

When things fall apart, the traditional ways of speaking about God do not always work. Herbert Levine argues that, at watershed moments in Judaism (e.g., the destruction of two Jerusalem temples in 587 BCE and 70 CE, the expulsion of the Jews from Spain in 1492, and the intense persecution and murder of Jews from 1933–1945), many psalms were "framed and reframed to respond to national catastrophe," revealing significant modifications in the way in which people believed and thought about God's power and role in history. These new under-standings of God found expression in writing and liturgy.[14]

In Psalms 22 and 71, the rupture experienced by the individual and/or community is evident in a new expression for God as Deliverer: the metaphor of God as Midwife. To view the Deliverer God who saves the believer from debilitating circumstances in terms of the female image of a midwife offers at least two intriguing interpretative possibilities for God's deliverance in contemporary situations of severe trauma.

First, the metaphor of God as Midwife in Psalm 22 and Psalm 71 fulfills an important role in the psalmist's understanding of who God is in times when nothing makes sense. Trauma causes people to experience dissonance, to question their place in the world and their relationship with the Divine. At such times, when the language system proves to be limited or inadequate, it may be necessary to find new kinds of speech. Especially in Psalm 22, we shall see how the metaphor of God as Midwife reverses death and denotes an unflinching commitment to life. As in the images of God as Mourner or Wailing Woman and God as Mother, the image of God as Midwife provides an incentive to broaden and transform our overall understanding of God in the direction of hope and new life.

Second, it is evident that memory plays an important role in the process of handling trauma. To invoke the image of God as Deliverer in a situation of anguish and despair is to recall memories of God's deliverance in the lives of our ancestors or in our own personal experience. However, it is also a question of *what* we choose to remember. The psalmists' recollection of God's acts of deliverance in the image of God as Midwife recalls memories that are quite different from the customary images of God as a Mighty Liberator-Warrior who kills or destroys, or as an Influential Redeemer who uses his patriarchal power and influence to effect change in the economic and socio-political sphere. The alternative memory of God as Midwife evokes the narrative of Israel's liberation from Egypt, the "muted voices" of the midwives Shiphrah and Puah, who continued to help the Hebrew women bear children (Exod. 1:15–22).[15] These muted voices evoke a different kind of Deliverer God, which affects the way we consider other people's role in our ongoing personal and communal struggles for liberation.

To understand the intriguing image of God as Divine Midwife in Psalm 22 and Psalm 71, let us first consider the paradigmatic story in Exodus 1 that contains memories of two midwives, Shiphrah and Puah.

MEMORIES OF MIDWIVES

The quintessential memory of midwives in Israel's imagination is most probably the story in Exodus of the two Hebrew (or Egyptian)[16] midwives Shiphrah and Puah. The story of their courage and unwavering commitment to outwit Pharaoh and to foster new life serves as a powerful symbol of ordinary people's ability to resist violence (Exod. 1:15–22).

The midwives' unflinching dedication to labor with mothers to bring children into the world and the intimate connection between mother and midwife offer us a lens through which to view the larger story of deliverance in the book of Exodus. Jacqueline Lapsley sees in the midwives and the other women who appear in Exodus 1–2 (Moses' mother and sister, and Pharaoh's daughter) a model of nonviolent resistance that stands in contrast to the violent for liberation effected by the men in the story—even by the main liberator(s), Moses (and God).[17] Lapsley describes the role of the women resisting empire as follows:

> The Hebrew and Egyptian women in the first two chapters, Shiphrah and Puah, and the unnamed others, take enormous risks transgressing traditionally rigid boundaries, especially of ethnicity and class, in order to form a cooperative network of care and nurture of those most vulnerable to violence.[18]

Employing double-voiced speech,[19] the midwives outwitted Pharaoh by drawing on his stereotypes of Hebrew women (they are like animals) in order to conceal their civil disobedience, their refusal to kill the male babies.[20] A rabbinic interpretation reflected in the midrash on Exodus offers an imaginative interpretation of their motivation: Modeling themselves on Abraham—even though he was willing to sacrifice his son—the midwives reason as follows: "Abraham, out of loving kindness, fed all passersby, regardless of their faith, and we are not only unable to provide the babies with food, but we've been ordered to murder them! No. We will keep them alive in any way we can (Exod. Rabbah 1:15)."

The midwives in this story of deliverance do not labor alone. Jochabed (Moses' mother), Pharaoh's daughter, and Miriam (Moses' sister) all continue the work started by the midwives by choosing life over death. In their respective ways, these women are mothers and surrogate mothers to the baby Moses, united by the overall objective of preserving life. The action of Pharaoh's daughter, pulling the baby from a certain watery grave, emulates the midwife's action of drawing the baby from the womb. Indeed, the Egyptian princess bestows a name on the baby with the root meaning in Hebrew "to draw up" (*mšh*), infusing an Egyptian name (Moses) with ironic significance (Exod. 2:10).[21]

Finally, the decision of the midwives (and the other women in Exod. 1–2) to protect those who are vulnerable foreshadows God's deliverance. According to Lapsley, "women's values" reflected in the "courageous boundary-crossing actions" of the female characters intent on preserving life eventually become the governing "divine values," pointing to the liberation of all people from the social, cultural, and political boundaries that confine them.[22]

These memories of the midwives are vulnerable; they easily disappear in the midst of the power struggles between those in charge. Eileen Schuller demonstrates how references to the midwives disappear in postbiblical literature. In the book of Jubilees, for example, the midwives vanish completely in the retelling of the Exodus story.[23] Moreover, Carole Fontaine argues that, in the healing traditions preserved in the biblical text, what is often missing from the "portrait of the healer is the presence of women who act in a healing capacity." In the portrayal of Jesus as healer, for instance, "the midwife, the wise woman, the folk healer, the mothers, wives, sisters, and daughters who routinely nurse the ailing members of the traditional household" are glaringly absent.[24] In this regard, it is imperative to reclaim the important role of midwives, mothers, and surrogate mothers in these ancient stories—"the women healing" who, as Elaine Wainwright argues, "appear only in the cracks, the spaces . . . and stereotypes" of these texts.[25] Although Wainwright is right in that healing in the biblical text is mostly "gendered male,"[26] I propose that the image of God as Midwife that found its way into the psalms presents us with the opportunity to reenvision or reimagine the conventional understanding of God as the One who delivers or heals by referring to the suppressed memories of midwives.

The image of the midwife powerfully communicates the commitment to preserve life in life-and-death situations. Singing their songs of lament from the edge of Sheol during the postexilic period, the people of Israel began to understand that the promise of deliverance would be delayed. They had to hope in a God who would bring about a new creation—a belief that is vividly portrayed in the role of a midwife who tirelessly works in difficult and often dangerous circumstances to bring life into this world. The image of a Divine Midwife and the memories of midwives offer some powerful perspectives on the image of God's deliverance that may speak to our own precarious circumstances of living too close to Sheol.

A NEW KIND OF SPEECH:
GOD AS MIDWIFE IN PSALM 22

"My God, my God, why have you forsaken me?" (Ps. 22:1). This anguished cry reflects the profound inner struggle of a person trying to reconcile her personal relationship with God ("my God") with her current experience of God's absence ("why have you forsaken me?").[27]

The psalmist dialogues with voices from the past and the present as she tries to recall who God is. Employing a variety of traditional metaphors to describe God, the psalmist is searching for language that will pull her out of her despair. She begs the God of her ancestors (v. 4), the Liberator God (vv. 4–5, 8, 20–21), the God of holiness (v. 3) to save her. Even the voices of those mocking the psalmist (v. 8) invoke these traditional understandings of God as they parody the ancestors' confidence in the God who saves.[28] Yet, these traditional descriptions of God bring no comfort. After evoking the traditionally cherished voices of the past (vv. 4–5), the psalmist draws a sharp contrast between her experience and the authoritative voices of tradition. At the beginning of verse 6, the psalmist uses the phrase "But I . . ." to introduce an outpouring of words of despair in verses 6–7. She utters her anguish and describes the shame of being dehumanized (v. 6), which is in contrast to her ancestors' experience (v. 5). Furthermore, the psalmist perceives that her ancestors trusted God and were saved, which is different from her own experience of a God who is absent and who does not deliver her from suffering despite her trust in God.

The psalmist seems to question the effectiveness of the authoritative voices of the past, because her despair negates them. The traditional symbolic system proves to be hopelessly inadequate in the current situation. The psalmist needs a new language, "a new symbolic order capable of encompassing the vastly expanded territory of the psalmist's experience."[29]

The psalm expresses the psalmist's transformation from absolute despair in verses 2–21 to a renewed hope for the future in verses 22–31, a change that is so radical that some scholars have suggested that this psalm originally consisted of two separate psalms. Most scholars now hold to the unity of the psalm and acknowledge that it provides a compelling example of moving from lament to praise. The psalm illustrates the dynamic process of moving from speaking in the voices of others to finding our own voice; that is, as Mikhail Bakhtin reminds us, transforming the authoritarian discourse of the past into an internally persuasive discourse.[30] Only when God-language becomes internally persuasive can the psalmist begin to imagine a transformed future.

Within this process, the less dominant female metaphor of God as Midwife (vv. 9–10) provides the first signs of a type of internally persuasive speech that can break open traditional formulations about God. The image of God as Midwife occurs in verses 9–10 as part of a motivational clause, similar to the motivational clause in verses 3–5, in which the psalmist provides reasons for asking for God's help. However, there is a distinct difference between the content of these two clauses. John Kselman describes this difference by means of the transition that occurs from "our fathers" (v. 3) to "my mother" (vv. 9–10); from the voices of the community to the individual's own experience.[31]

In contrast to the traditional voices of the ancestors, the motivational clause in verses 9–10 is marked by personal, intimate language and describes the psalmist's experience of God being present from the moment she drew her first breath. The psalmist addresses God with the personal pronoun "you," saying that God was the one who assisted at her birth, who drew[32] her out of her mother's womb and who kept her safe on her mother's breasts. From that moment on she was cast upon

God, whom she boldly calls "*my* God." Verses 9–10 end with a statement of faith ("You are my God"), transforming the initial cry of despair in verse 1 ("My God, my God, why have you forsaken me?") into a declaration of trust.

Immediately after this metaphor of God as Midwife in verses 9–10, one finds the first petition in which the psalmist begs God not to be far away from her (v. 11). This petition is repeated in verse 19 with the added request to God to deliver her from her plight (vv. 20–21). These two petitions form an *inclusio*, framing the honest and painful expression of the believer's suffering. After the second petition, Psalm 22 transforms dramatically to express hope (vv. 22–31). The move from the traditional voices of the fathers to the personal experience of the speaker, in which the female metaphor of God as Midwife plays a central role, introduces this transformation.

This divine metaphor of God as Midwife moreover captures the precarious nature of the believer's situation and envisions an active means of moving forward. Women often died in childbirth (see Rachel in Gen. 35:16–19); many still do. Therefore, the midwife fulfills an important function in those moments when death and life intersect.[33] God draws the psalmist from the pit (see also Ps. 30:3), evoking the image of a midwife who draws a baby from the womb. Should the child remain in the womb, the mother and the child would die; similarly, the psalmist pleads with God to bring life into her situation of suffering and despair. In verses 20–21, the psalmist once more uses the traditional metaphor of God as Deliverer when she begs God to save her life. But now this metaphor does not constitute anymore the authoritarian voices of others but has been reclaimed by the psalmist to become internally persuasive. By employing the female metaphor of God as Midwife with its connotations of delivery from a life-and-death situation, the psalmist enriches the traditional metaphor of God as Deliverer.

The metaphor of God as Midwife moreover occurs in the midst of suffering and despair. This divine portrayal does not offer a magic cure. Immediately before and after this image, the psalmist describes her physical and psychological anguish. She speaks of being persecuted. Using a series of animal metaphors (bulls in v. 12, a lion in v. 13, dogs in v. 16), the psalmist describes being threatened, surrounded, or trapped by her circumstances. Additionally, the psalmist describes the severe physical symptoms she experiences from the psychological anguish. This reaches a climax in verse 14, as the psalmist portrays, in rich figurative language, how she feels like water poured out, her bones separated and her heart like melting wax.

In the midst of this despair, the psalmist pairs the metaphor of God as Midwife with another female image, that of God as Mother. Phyllis Trible notes how in Psalm 22 the "divine and the maternal intertwine."[34] "Subject has become object; divine midwife has become divine mother. To be kept safe upon the breasts of the mother is to be cast upon God from the womb."[35]

The metaphor of God as Midwife who works with God as the Nurturing Mother describes God's presence in the midst of the reality of suffering. Wendy Farley has written extensively about the compassion that causes God to enter into suffering. God's presence is evident in the psalmist's repeated petition, "Do not be far away." But Farley rightly points out that God is not "the benevolent but impotent deity who 'suffers with the world.'" Rather, "divine compassion is . . . a radical love that offers liberating power" to overcome the forces of chaos that are responsible for suffering in the world.[36] So in verses 19–22, the psalmist not only asks God to be *present*, she asks God to *change* her situation. This twofold function of God's nurturing presence and saving power is captured in the metaphor of God as Midwife, who is both present and active for change that results in new life.

REDEEMING MEMORIES:
GOD AS MIDWIFE IN PSALM 71

Psalm 71 is a powerful prayer that creates space for remembrance. In the depths of despair, persecution, hurt, and shame, the believer keeps on praying, employing—as Carroll Stuhlmueller suggests—"the language of the ancient psalms, which have become part of bone and blood."[37] Psalm 71 draws on other psalms of lament and thanksgiving in its composition (see, e.g., the correspondence between vv. 1–3 and Ps. 31:1–3a; vv. 5–6 and Ps. 22:9–10; v. 12a and Ps. 22:1, 11, 19; v. 12b and Ps. 38:22 and 40:13; v. 13 and Ps. 35:4, 26; v. 18 and Ps. 22:30–31; v. 19 and Ps. 36:6).[38] The reuse of previous prayers draws on the theme of memory and its role in rebuilding life, which was previously introduced as an important aspect of coming to terms with trauma.

This process of remembering is complex and ambiguous. In verse 20, the believer vacillates between praying to God for deliverance and holding God responsible for the calamities that have befallen him: "You who have made me see many troubles and calamities will revive me again; from the depths of the earth you will bring me up again." In this ambiguous statement it is evident that the psalmist wrestles with the age-old issue of the relationship between God and suffering. The honest memories of the believer's suffering and resistance that hold on to God's righteous deeds in the past, seeking to right the wrongs of this world, constitute the first steps to repair a broken world. These memories attest to a well-developed personal relationship with God and the growing emphasis on prayer in the postexilic period as a means of creating a meaningful existence in the midst of a deeply threatening situation.[39]

The metaphor of God as Midwife (v. 6), and its associations with birth and new life, has the potential to reshape and expand our understanding of what it means to say that God is the Deliverer God. The metaphor of God as Midwife is found amid a series of verbs that typically denote God's deliverance by way of military feats. Verbs such as "deliver" (*nṣl*), "rescue" (*plṭ*) and "save" (*yšʿ*), as well as references to impenetrable places (such as "sheltering rock," "rock," and "fortress") may have developed from descriptions of military conflict (see the repeated reference to enemies in vv. 10–11, 13) that were extended to include other contexts of danger (see also rescue from wild animals or redemption from debt slavery in v. 23).[40] At first glance, the language of birth and new life seems out of place in this military-oriented context. However, this language contributes to the transformation of the memory of God as Deliverer into a redeeming memory; in particular, it relates to the overall objective of creating life-giving connections with other people.

First, this metaphor of God as Midwife is a good example of the dynamic nature of theology that reuses traditions but also creatively actualizes existing traditions in innovative ways. So the verb that is used to describe God's deliverance as Midwife in Psalm 22:10 is *gḥy*— from *gyḥ/gwḥ* ("burst forth/draw forth"; see also Job 38:8), and refers to the action of pulling a baby from its mother's womb. In Psalm 71:6, though, the verb that describes God's involvement in freeing the baby from the mother's womb is *gōzī*, an uncertain term that may be derive from the root *gzh* ("cut off/sever"), suggesting that God has "cut" or "severed" the infant from its mother's womb.[41]

The language of "severing" or "cutting loose" may explain the duties of a midwife who, in a situation where both mother and baby would otherwise die for certain, cuts open the mother's womb to free the baby.

The reference to this harsh action captures the vulnerability of the speaker, who is in a life-threatening position. James Crenshaw formulates the believer's condition as follows: "Trapped in the turbulent waters of the depths, the psalmist prays to be extracted from the jaws of death."[42]

Second, in the context of God's acts of deliverance, the metaphor of God as Midwife suggests the notion of birth or rebirth. In the midst of severe trauma it is an important realization for the survivor to claim, "I am still here. I am still alive." Praying to God as Midwife evokes this emphasis on life, particularly after a person has looked death in the eye (v. 20). The midwife metaphor resonates with the strong yearning for life that is evident in trauma survivors. Keshgegian notes that she was struck by "the thirst of life" she encountered among the trauma survivors she interviewed. Though Keshgegian admits that survivors' courage is often accompanied by tremendous doubts, the yearning for life is still responsible for their desire to create a new life for themselves. She writes, "Yet they go on, most of them, most of the time, and they choose life, most of them, most of the time."[43]

Third, despite their yearning to live, trauma survivors recognize what Keshgegian calls "the persistence of an unhealed wound." Thus, even though they continue to live, life is often "layered on top of the wounds."[44] The particular manifestation of the metaphor of God as Midwife in Psalm 71:6 manages to hold together this tension of life in the midst of death. The connotations of the very real danger of infantile and maternal death during childbirth allow the believer to face the severity of his situation. The act of "severing" or "cutting loose" is suggestive of the mother's death and further serves to emphasize the deeply traumatized nature of the believer's experience. However, with the affirmation in verse 20 that God pulls the believer out of the depths of the deep, the midwife imagery captures the believer's experience of escaping certain death through rebirth. Keshgegian notes that trauma survivors can face the reality of death and loss when there is an emphasis on "rebirth"—when continuing to live is the best possible revenge.[45]

Fourth, the metaphor of God as Midwife is an image of power, denoting specifically the power to give life or to rescue life from death. The midwife works ceaselessly to bring life into the world, often in treacherous circumstances, as illustrated by the memory of Shiphrah and Puah who, in the face of danger, labored with expectant mothers to deliver their babies (Exod. 1). Invoking the metaphor of God as

Midwife highlights God's profound commitment to life. The conviction that God is the God of life, who works ceaselessly to bring life into the world, forms the basis of the psalmist's prayer to the Deliverer God.

The depiction of God as Deliverer who powerfully steps in and delivers the baby does not eliminate the agency of the mother. In normal childbirth, the mother still has to struggle to bring the baby into the world, moving it from darkness into light, from possible death to life. This agency of the mother points to the role of people who are called to serve as God's partners, to work tirelessly toward liberation. However, in the case of human failure, as in the mother's inability to deliver the baby, the midwife's act of slitting open the womb suggests that God as Midwife may take drastic measures in order to free a child from death.

Finally, this metaphor offers possibilities for renewed life connections, which (according to Keshgegian) form an essential part of transforming memories of suffering and redemption into truly redeeming memories. After delivery, a newborn needs care (being cleaned, fed, sheltered, and protected). The image of a child captures the tenuous situation of the believer who prays for God's comforting presence in verse 21: "You will increase my honor, embrace me, and comfort me once again" (Crenshaw's translation). The meaning of the verb *sbb*, which precedes the verb "to comfort" (*nhm*), is unclear. It could mean "to turn around," as reflected in the NRSV's translation: "once again" (see the JPS translation of God who will "turn and comfort me"). Alternatively, this verb may mean to surround or embrace, as reflected in Crenshaw's translation above.[46] This notion of God "surrounding" or "embracing" the believer offers an interesting feature to the image of God as Deliverer. In the psalms, "surrounding" typically is a threatening image that refers to enemies and/or animals (see also Ps. 22:13, 17 [MT]). In Psalm 71, however, the act of surrounding represents comforting and fits well with the connotations of a helpless child in need of care and support. It thus seems that liberation does not end with the act of redemption, but that survival depends on the cultivation of meaningful relationships based on comfort and support. Particularly if the mother dies in childbirth, caregivers or surrogate mothers are vital for the child's survival. The community is obliged to take responsibility for caring for one another; the image of God as Deliverer thus finds extension in the life of community.

BECOMING MIDWIVES

In a world where everything seems terribly unsettled, the psalms of lament speak with new force. These psalms acknowledge that the world is fragile and fraught with chaos. People are prone to both natural and human disasters; disease and acts of terror or war can destroy all that we hold dear. We are much more fragile than we think.

Taking our cue from the psalms of lament, our cries to the Deliverer God resound individually and collectively. The image of God as Midwife not only offers us the language to pull us from the pit of despair but also markedly changes the way we think of God as Deliverer. The Midwife metaphor is a deeply personal image that portrays a God who acts, a God who is willing and able to change our circumstances. At the height of the pain, in the midst of the anguish at what seems to be labor without end, we need a God who is not distant but who is present in our pain. We need a God who offers us comfort in our travail and who is willing to reach into the womb and pull the baby out into the light. The metaphor of God as Midwife attests to the fact that God is resolutely on the side of life, working hard to allow new life to enter this world.

One of the underlying assumptions of this book, in which I seek to find different ways of speaking about the Deliverer God, is the belief that our language for God affects human behavior. Inspired by the metaphor of God as Midwife and the memories of the midwives that linger in the background, we are encouraged to reconsider our own vocation as midwives in this world of ours, in which people may increasingly be in need of healing. Rabbi Arthur Waskow's poem "Why Exodus Is Not Enough" expresses this notion of human midwives emulating and continuing the work of the Divine Midwife:

> When the midwives Shifrah and Puah
> Saved the children that Pharaoh ordered them to kill,
> That was the beginning of the birth-time;
> When Pharaoh's daughter joined with Miriam
> To give a second birth to Moses from the waters
> She birthed herself anew into God's daughter, Bat-yah
> And our people turned to draw ourselves toward life
> When God became our Midwife
> And named us Her firstborn,
> Though we were the smallest and youngest of the peoples,
> The birthing began;
> When the waters of the Red Sea broke,

We were delivered
So tonight it is our task to help the Midwife
Who tonight is giving birth to a new people—
And so to give a new birth to ourselves.[47]

In a world where despair, hatred, greed, malice, violence, and abuse of power seem almost unbearable, we need more people to take up the vocation of midwife. We need individuals who, like Pharaoh's daughter, cross ethnic and racial and socio-economic divisions with the singular purpose of effecting God's deliverance in the lives of others. Instead of more violence, greed, and self-centeredness, we need women and men who work diligently to bring life into situations of darkness and despair, working selflessly for the good of the most vulnerable, serving as midwives for peace and justice.

Icons like Nelson Mandela, Desmond Tutu, Albertina Sisulu, Martin Luther King Jr., Rosa Parks, Dorothy Height, Mohandas Gandhi, and many others have been called to be midwives for peace, justice, and reconciliation; agents of change driven by the impulse to do good and to bring life into this world that is filled with darkness and despair.[48] However, not only these bright shining stars are called to act as midwives. The point of the story in Exodus is that ordinary human beings, wherever they are, can make a difference. As Sharon Welch argues,

> Some people do find their life work in building and sustaining creativity and respect: nurses and doctors giving considerate care, teachers challenging and respecting students, some employers pay their workers fairly and encourage participation, job safety, and environmental responsibility. Injustice is challenged: child labor laws are enforced; some people and governments resisted the Holocaust; apartheid was overthrown and a new social order is in the process of being built.[49]

This belief that individuals can effect change through simple acts of selfless love, to reconstitute the world, is something that is embodied in the Jewish concept of *Tiqqun Olam*—restoring the world. Paul Hanson notes, "repairing the universe through acts of loving kindness taught by Jewish rabbinical tradition, is not a task reserved for the Messiah. It is the vocation of every friend of mercy and justice that strengthens the partnership between God and humanity . . . in this relationship alone lies hope for a more peaceful and humane future."[50]

Chapter 5

God's Delivering Presence

In the year 2001, on the brilliantly clear morning of Tuesday, September 11, I saw the divine presence. She was squatting in the midst of billowing smoke and raging fire, of mountains of twisted steel and broken glass. An apocalypse of destruction and terror engulfed her. Her face, bearing the serene features of an indigenous woman of this continent, was covered with a thick layer of ash. But the ashen face seemed strangely glistening. The divine presence wept. And then I saw: in her strong brown arms she was gathering the remains of her beautiful creation, all the maimed and the burnt, the dying and the dead, the unborn, the orphaned, the lost, and those who inflicted loss. I saw her gather, passionately and gently, the lives of all. With tears trickling down her ashen face, she caught in her arms those who jumped from great heights, and she cradled in the palm of her hand a dying priest. And the divine presence whispered, Holy, holy, holy is every human life. Heaven and earth and the very heart

80

of God mourn when death so violently overcomes life. Then I said, Woe is me! Why do my eyes have to see the divine presence mourning, gathering her torn creation in her arms? Why can I not see God sitting on a throne, high and lofty, with the train of his garment filling the temple and seraphs in attendance above him, each with six wings? I am lost. Then one of the living dead came to me and touched my eyes. Look again, he said. And I saw the divine presence, groaning, crouched amid the heaps of rubble, her belly large and full of life. And I saw that she was a woman in travail, desperate to birth new life, a child of peace. And as every mother since the first, the divine presence also birthed amid waves of pain, and in fear of futility. Then I heard the voice of the divine presence saying, Who will labor with me, and who will be midwife to life? Here I am, I said, I want to birth life with you. And the divine presence said, Come, take your place beside me.

Teresa Berger, "Fragments of a Vision in a September 11 World."[1]

CONJURING UP A NEW WORLD

In her striking meditation "Fragments of a Vision in a September 11 World," Teresa Berger beautifully brings together the three metaphors for God featured in this book. Berger illustrates movingly how the metaphors of a God as Mourner, Mother in Labor, and Midwife offer resources to speak to a deeply wounded world. In her meditation, Berger expresses the heartfelt desire to see a sovereign, mighty manifestation of God—a transcendent God sitting on a throne—an image from the book of Isaiah that radiates holiness, order, and wholeness. However, the author senses that the reality of this most desperate of situations necessitates a different language for God. The metaphors of God as Mourner, Mother, and Midwife in Berger's meditation express something of the unfathomable pain people experience in the midst of horror, destruction, and death—as well as the first glimmerings of hope for a new life.

What makes these images in Berger's meditation so compelling is their ability to conjure up another world. In his treatment of the "suffering servant" in Isaiah 53, David Clines writes of the potential of language to create "another set of principles, values, relationships, and perceptions, which then confronts the reader."[2] This new world and new way of seeing challenge the reader to transform old perceptions and to adopt new visions of what may be.

In the previous chapters, I have explored how the metaphors of God as Mourner, Mother, and Midwife—which were formulated during Israel's trauma-filled experience during and after the Babylonian exile—may contribute to the formation of an alternative way for understanding God. With the help of such an understanding, people can deal constructively with their pain and, eventually, begin to see new possibilities. In the midst of situations around the world of ethnic strife, economic collapse, disease, disasters, human rights violations, war, and terror that destroy people's lives, this alternative understanding of the Deliverer God that we gain from the metaphors of God as Mourner, Mother, and Midwife may present resources not only to survive but also to take up the task of living.

When we think of God's delivering presence in those instances when everything seems hopeless, we may turn to a wealth of theological reflection that emerged during one of the darkest, most desperate times in recorded human history: the Holocaust. "Auschwitz"—the name of one of the concentration camps established in Poland during World War II—has become a symbol or synecdoche for the entire Holocaust and the theological struggle to make sense of God's involvement (or absence) during the deportation, persecution, and killing of six million Jews as well as countless others whom Nazi Germany deemed undesirable.

Numerous people who have reflected on Auschwitz have said that it is impossible to speak of liberation in the midst of the horrors of these death camps. Yet, this is the task that Melissa Raphael sets herself in her provocative book *The Female Face of God in Auschwitz*.[3] Raphael wants us to think differently about the notion of redemption or deliverance—an objective very much at the heart of this book, too. By focusing on women's simple acts of washing and caring for themselves and others in the death camps, Raphael moves toward a theology of God's presence as she argues that it is in the cleansed face of the other that we see the female face of God. This theological construction is based on the lives of ordinary women, and it resonates with the Jewish tradition of the Shekhinah, the female presence of God, who is said to have gone into exile with Israel and suffered with her people.[4] According to rabbinic tradition, the female presence of God is with Israel when they are unclean (*Yoma* 56b). The Shekhinah watches over them when they are sick (*Shabbat* 12b), and she hurts when they are in pain (*Sanhedrin* 46a).[5]

Raphael's constructive theology dethrones the male patriarchal construct of the omnipotent God that many people have found inadequate in dealing with the Holocaust. Her theology of presence—like the metaphors of God as Mourner, Mother, and Midwife—contributes to a theology of God's presence that offers redemptive potential in the most difficult of times. Flora Keshgegian proposes that women's experiences of embodiment, of being pregnant, giving birth, nursing, and raising children can be fruitfully appropriated to portray an awareness of God's presence and personal involvement in people's lives.[6] Drawing on this theology of presence, in the rest of this chapter I will suggest ways in which developing an alternative understanding of God ought to transform our practices. I will discuss in particular the importance of education as transformation; a process that African American scholar bell hooks calls a "pedagogy of hope."[7]

Finally, I will offer alternative ways of portraying God's deliverance in expressions of worship. The theological language that draws on the tears cried by the wailing women, the nurturing actions of mothers, and the skill and engagement of the midwives committed to bringing forth new life may be employed in a worship setting in order to provide people with the resources to survive as well as with the impetus to transform their daily lives.

TOWARD A THEOLOGY OF PRESENCE

Melissa Raphael's feminist theological reconstruction traces God's redemptive and immanent presence in Auschwitz and challenges the traditional model of an omnipotent, omniscient [male] God who exerts full control over the world. In the context of the Holocaust, the patriarchal construction of an all-powerful God collapsed on itself. Raphael argues that this model of an omnipotent, controlling God grew into something unmanageable, like a "golem . . . a soulless clay servant . . . conjured by patriarchy's own will to usurp or exploit the power of its creator." She explains that, according to legend, Elija Ball Shem, Rabbi of Chelm, created a golem to be his servant, but it eventually grew so large that he could no longer control it. "[W]hen it dissolved back into the mud the rabbi was crushed and submerged under its weight." Raphael concludes, "This is a parable of the monarchical God of Auschwitz."[8]

But Raphael takes on not only the theological construction of patriarchal Judaism; she also critiques fellow post-Holocaust thinkers like Emmanuel Levinas, Martin Buber, and Eliezer Berkovits, who have all argued for some form of God's hiddenness to explain God's silence during the Holocaust.[9] Yet, Raphael argues, citing the example of the mother of two ten-year-old twin girls, Nellie and Vlodka Blit, who managed to house her daughters with a Gentile family in Warsaw and would walk by their house every day so that the two girls could see her from their window, "Presence, a keeping watch, is a function of love. A present God paces back and forth, circling the object of her concern; an absent God seems to have walked away."[10]

An equally disconcerting image for God to emerge in post-Holocaust thinking regards the notion of the abusive God. Just like the image of a deserting God, the image of an abusive God jeopardizes a meaningful relationship with God, particularly among people who have survived abuse or abandonment. David Blumenthal recounts an interview with a survivor of abuse who declared that she could not worship an omnipotent, remote, uncaring God. She said she would "stay as far away from Him as possible. He would not be deserving of my company, comfort, praise, and love."[11] Elie Wiesel saw such a God in the eyes of a twelve-year-old girl whom the German officers kept in their barracks at Auschwitz for their pleasure. Wiesel writes about seeing this girl while he was a prisoner at Auschwitz: "Suddenly she turned her darkened eyes toward me: God was still in them. The God of chaos and impotence. The God who tortures twelve-year-old children."[12]

Raphael counters this imagery of an omnipotent, abusive God by reimagining God's intimate presence in the stories of ordinary women who, through the exceedingly personal and ordinary acts of caring for their own bodies or the bodies of others, reflected something of the presence of God. These "simple acts of humanity" had the purpose of restoring the personhood that was seriously imperiled by the dehumanizing Nazis death camps. And, as Raphael says, "God is present wherever personhood is honoured."[13]

Relying on memoirs of Holocaust survivors, Raphael tells stories that are representative of the countless unknown women whose resistance to inhumanity through random acts of kindness across biological and familial ties serve as a powerful model for God's "feeding, clothing, and saving presence" in Auschwitz. Raphael notes that virtually all women in Auschwitz formed surrogate families: women adopting children, children adopting mothers—these friendships and quasi-familial relationships played a key role in their will to survive. Raphael recounts a story told by Sara Nomberg-Przytyk, who was on the verge of death from exposure during a forced march from Auschwitz when a nameless woman gave her own blanket to Sara, saying that she would share with her daughter. When Sara repeatedly asked for her name, the woman told her to stretch out her hand, and placed a crust of bread in it.[14]

This ethic of solidarity was also at work in the Auschwitz women's acts of care for their bodies; their almost ritualized acts of purification that made the world fit for the divine presence. By washing, these women engaged in active resistance against the humiliation and degradation they experienced at the hands of the Nazis.[15] In this regard, Raphael also recounts a poignant recollection by Olga Lengyel:

> No spectacle was more comforting than that provided by the women when they undertook to cleanse themselves thoroughly in the evening. They passed the single scrubbing brush to one another with a firm determination to resist dirt and the lice. That was our only way of waging war against the parasites, against our jailers, and against every force that made us its victims.[16]

One of the rather shocking images of God's presence in Auschwitz has to do with the notion of God being present even in the midst of the most vile, profane circumstances that marked the death camps. Raphael notes that Deuteronomy 23:13–14 makes special arrangements for Israel to dispose of their excrement while journeying through the wilderness. The reason for this was the underlying assumption that the camp ought to be kept holy in order to ensure God's presence. As verse 14 plainly states, if God were to "see anything indecent among you" God would "turn away from you." In Auschwitz, conditions were abhorrent to say the least. Based on women's memoirs about "the gross indignities of bodily degradation," Raphael describes in gruesome detail the diarrhea due to typhus and other ailments, the lack of opportunities and facilities to wash themselves. A theology of presence that places God in the midst of such vile conditions thus offers a serious overturning of the abovementioned tradition, positing that God is present in the midst of "her soiled creation." As Raphael argues, "God knew Israel's 'unseemliness' but still moved about the camp and did not turn away. Indeed she was like a mother who will not be repelled by her child's 'unseemliness,' but in washing her must come all the closer because of it."[17]

Even in death, the female presence of being there for others, of being a comfort to the last, points toward God's presence in the most desperate of times, as the dying cared for the dying.[18] One story that Raphael recounts makes this point particularly well: "a nameless old woman with 'hair white as snow' . . . [was] holding in her arms a motherless 1-year-old child as she stood at the edge of the communal pit, about to be shot with the rest of her village by Nazi troops. The old woman sang to the child and tickled him under the chin until he laughed with joy. Then they were shot."[19]

The stories from Auschwitz reveal numerous examples of women who "showed compassion to those even more broken than themselves." It is in these acts of kindness that God's presence was revealed in the camp: "It was their acts that were representative of God for all women, for the imitation of God brings God among us."[20]

God's deliverance in a place such as Auschwitz is thus understood in terms of God's delivering presence. God's deliverance does not consist of a divine warrior intervening to smite the enemy and to free the captives, but rather in the small salvific acts in the midst of pain and suffering that offer the possibility of redemption. Thus we see in the writings of Anne Frank and Etty Hillesum, who died in Auschwitz, the conviction that God saves people "*in* but not *from* the terror in which they live and die." For Frank and Hillesum, "kindness was redemptive—kindness was a precondition of the world's moral restoration."[21] These small acts of relational care, both human and divine, though not omnipotent in nature, proved to be indestructible, as evidenced in the witness of women whose words survived beyond their fragile bodies.[22]

The metaphors of God as Mourner, Mother, and Midwife place God in the very midst of people's everyday struggles, even at the most desperate of times. The Divine Mourner cries over the pain of her people, feeling the loss of loved ones in her own body. The Divine Mother serves as a powerful way to speak about God's presence in a way that does not negate the messiness of life—the diarrhea and vomit that form a less than pleasant part of a mother's involvement with her child are used to communicate God's presence in the worst, most vile, and inhumane circumstances. The Divine Midwife is present with those who are suffering; her hands are covered in blood, and her healing, helping presence conceivably makes the difference between life and death. To think of God as Deliverer in terms of these particular female metaphors that place God in the midst of people's suffering may be helpful to people who are struggling to survive, giving them the strength to persevere.

Thinking in terms of God's delivering presence helps us to think differently about God's power. According to Flora Keshgegian, God's presence is revealed not through mighty acts, but in and through the small, ordinary actions of individuals and groups that make life possible. "God's sovereignty may be re-imagined as God's energy, present and active, in history, rather than God's absolute and determinative dominion over the outcome."[23] Keshgegian defines God's "might" not with reference to conquest and victory, but to the ongoing, simple acts of life-giving or giving dignity to the dying. "To speak of God's power as mighty is to proclaim that the divine is on the side of life, but not to talk of victories or final triumphs, or of goodness being realized fully."[24]

The metaphors of God as Mourner, Mother, and Midwife, which place God in the midst of the brokenness and despair of our fragile lives, acknowledge that there are no quick fixes, magic cures, or guaranteed happy endings. Instead, these small acts of kindness are done step-by-step, out of a commitment to the good, without necessarily seeing the end. Keshgegian formulates this view as follows: "As long as there is life on earth, there is hope. Redemption is in and through life sustaining life."[25]

The wailing woman weeps her tears and encourages us to weep with her, even though we do not know whether there will be laughter and wholeness again. The mother gives birth to children and cares for them through their illnesses and tantrums, not knowing the kind of adults they will turn out, or even whether they will survive. The midwife acts in good faith that a baby will be born healthy, even though she is not sure whether her actions will have a positive outcome. All three of these metaphors view God's deliverance in terms of God's enduring and hopeful presence and give us a language to speak about the God who is on the side of life, who is present in the midst of the pain, without having to proclaim definitive outcomes and ultimate victories.

We have seen in the women's acts of kindness and compassion in Auschwitz how God's power is revealed exactly where people work for the good of others. Viewed in this way, we share God's work; all our actions become important as we claim our own role as partners in God's redemptive action: "God can only do her restorative work in and with those who care" and labor beside her.[26]

This understanding is also at the heart of Sharon Welch's ethic of solidarity—that people are "empowered by a recognition of the power of divine love and healing at work in our communities of resistance." According to Welch, "Our efforts are partial, yet they are divine in their love and courage. They bear witness to the transcendent, healing power of love; they bear witness to the beauty and wonder of life."[27] Even though our work may be limited, fragmented, and in some instances seemingly futile, these acts of care and kindness are at the core of what it means to be human, and they illustrate that "the power of compassion is divine."[28]

The female metaphors of God as Mourner, Mother, and Midwife presume an intricate link between theology and ethics; between our particular theological vision and human ethical behavior. This is exemplified in a rabbinic writing urging imitation of God's acts of compassion: clothing the naked, visiting the sick, and comforting the mourners (*Sotah* 14a).[29] The metaphor of God as Wailing Woman roots the divine image in the brokenness of the world that calls us to action. We are called to serve as wailing women in our respective communities, to feel the pain of those around us, to lament the injustice that is responsible for the pain, and by means of our tears to resist whatever infringes on life. The metaphor of God as Mother inspires us to take up the vocation of reaching across biological and familial ties to include each and every person in need of nurture and care. In a broad sense of mothering, we are challenged to preserve life, to protect the weak and vulnerable, and to work for justice in the name of love. And, joining the actions of the Divine Midwife, we are called to serve as midwives in the world to help realize God's deliverance in the lives of others, working ceaselessly for change and justice and healing.

There are still many questions left unanswered when we contemplate how to speak about God's deliverance with reference to the manifold possible situations of pain and suffering. Reimagining the Deliverer God in terms of unconventional metaphors such as God as Mourner, Mother, and Midwife is most certainly open to critique. In *The Female Face of God in Auschwitz*, Raphael admits that critics might say that her proposal of viewing God's delivering presence in Auschwitz in terms of the maternal actions of washing and caring for one another can no more reconcile a loving God with human suffering than can patriarchal theology. Yet, a theological construction that places God in the midst of the violence and human misery has the distinct benefit of bringing God close to God's creation without multiplying or increasing terror.[30]

Another critique of the theology of an immanent, comforting God is its perceived ineffectiveness, as expressed in the following example: "If I were at the bottom of a deep pit, aching, cold, and nursing a broken arm, what I want and urgently need is a Rescuer with a very bright light and a long ladder, full of strength, joy, and assurance, who can get me out of the pit, not a god who sits in the darkness suffering with me."[31]

But a swift resolution, a happy ending, and a return to normalcy are seldom realistic. In the darkest moments, God's delivering presence in the form of care and kindness offered by other people is a source of hope, very much like the light of a (Sabbath) candle that pierces the darkness may serve as a reminder of God's presence.

Moreover, metaphors of God as Mother, Midwife, and Mourner should not be romanticized. From experience we know that mothers are not perfect; they lose patience, they become weary, and they can be petty, manipulative, and capricious. Raphael cites several examples of mothers in Auschwitz who deserted their children in order to save their own lives.[32] Nor is the image of the midwife above critique. Raphael recalls chilling accounts of doctors who would kill babies at birth in order to allow the mothers to survive, because with a newborn infant they were doomed to certain death.[33] The wailing woman image is open to abuse and manipulation. For example, the professional keeners who were hired to weep for money cast a shadow of doubt on the overall sincerity of the profession of the wailing woman. These instances of the negative dimension of the particular metaphors are a good reminder of the limitations of using human imagery for the Divine. Human beings are limited and flawed; inevitably, the human language and images we use to describe God follow suit. Yet, as we have seen in this book, these particular metaphors manage to capture something of God and God's relationship with people at their most vulnerable in a way that expresses God's liberating presence in a powerful way.

Finally, as I noted in chapter 1, when we use female imagery or language in our theological discourse, it is vital to avoid narrow gender constructions. Raphael, for instance, points to more than one example where males took on the task of maternal care.[34] Nor should female imagery for God be subjected to stereotypes of female passivity. None of the female images for God that were introduced in this book are passive. Instead, all of them are powerful, speaking of courage, strength, kindness, resourcefulness, and skill.

EDUCATION AS TRANSFORMATION

This constructive act of theological imagination in which we have engaged thus far is not an end in itself. The ethical implications outlined above are indicative of the fact that the purpose of feminist theological enterprise is to transform the world, to change the way people think and act. Elizabeth

Johnson summarizes her objectives to include "empowering women in the struggle for their own freedom and dignity" as well as encouraging the church "to grow as a living community of memory and hope, and promoting the transformation of church and society in accord with God's compassionate justice and care."[35]

But where do we start? As pastors, educators, parents, and theologians, we are indeed called to teach. In her book *Teaching Community: A Pedagogy of Hope,* bell hooks outlines her vision for what she calls "transformative education"—that seeks to align the world as it currently is to the world as it could be. She cites the essay of a medical doctor, Rachel Naomi Remen, who teaches medical students to integrate practices of compassion in their work as doctors. Remen says, "As educators, we cannot heal the shadow of our culture educating people to succeed in society as it is. We must have the courage to educate people to heal this world into what it might become."[36]

From hooks' work it is clear that teaching is deeply rooted in hope. Inspired by Paulo Freire's work, hooks writes, "Hopefulness empowers us to continue our work for justice even as the forces of injustice may gain greater power for a time. As teachers we enter the classroom with hope."[37] Within this educational process, I want to highlight the following three important practices that relate to this project's objective to communicate an alternative understanding of the Deliverer God.

Memory and Hope

The first step in a transformative education is to cultivate practices of remembrance that may serve as sources of hope. The muted voices of God as Mourner, Mother, and Midwife recall many hidden and even lost memories. To remember these lesser-known metaphors for God and to show how these metaphors impact the traditional understanding of God as Deliverer have an important educational function. Elizabeth Johnson, for example, discusses the importance of recalling women's memories of suffering, survival, and agency in an account such as the story of Hagar in Genesis 16 and 21, which the dominant voice of tradition has rendered nearly inaudible:[38]

> Recovering the lost memory of her creative striving to survive interrupts the dominant discourse. It demands that the corporate memory of the *ekklesia* make room for the female, the foreigner, the one in servitude, the religious stranger—and the person who is all four—as a vital player in the history of humanity with God. By

bringing Hagar visibly into the cloud of witnesses, it lifts up a source of lament and resistance as well as strength and inspiration for all who remember her name.[39]

Johnson suggests that, by remembering these lost memories and muted voices, today we are able to tell the story differently, expanding and reconceptualizing the traditional story line to make room for real women to exist as subjects in their own right.[40] Similarly, by introducing alternative metaphors for God, we engage in the important theological endeavor of allowing God's redemptive presence to alter the way we think about human relationships.

The memories of wailing women, mothers, and midwives that depict God's delivering presence serve as a source of hope. The purpose of recalling the painful memories of suffering and the stories of resistance and survival is ultimately "for the sake of human flourishing and life abundant beyond surviving."[41] In this way, remembering becomes a means for those who are trapped in traumatic situations to transcend their suffering in order to start seeing possibilities of new life in the here and now.

An important function of a transformative education is, then, to help students and parishioners to imagine these liberating possibilities that offer an alternative to a world of pain, oppression, and injustice. Without the capacity to imagine it would be difficult to speak of hope. This book is an attempt to imagine alternative possibilities that may help traumatized people to imagine life differently, to journey from injury and trauma to new life. Moreover, these unconventional metaphors for God offer alternative ways of being that resist those powers that seek to oppress and destroy.

Teaching Critical Thinking

A second practice that informs this project is the vital importance of teaching critical thinking. Flora Keshgegian argues that "Christianity and Christian theology need to be problematized in order to discern what does and does not contribute to salvation."[42] I have found that, by showing examples—from both my South African and my American contexts—of how God-language has been used (and quite often abused) in popular culture and in the public sphere, I am able to help students grow in awareness of the power of metaphors to shape a particular worldview and of the fact that these metaphors may have exceedingly harmful consequences.

Students can learn to reflect critically on traditional formulations regarding God and to explore imagery that depicts God as relational, kind, and compassionate. They can evaluate various metaphors to describe a God who may be imaged with reference to both male and female imagery, reflecting the notion that both male and female are created in God's image (Gen. 1:26). As a result of this critical thinking about God-language, students and parishioners may begin to explore alternative ways of looking at God and at the world around them.

Underlying this study is the hope that we can help create a society built on justice and mercy, a society that transcends sexism and racism, homophobia, and all the other "isms" that mar our world. As long as there are places where people are devalued as human beings based on prejudices of gender, color, sexuality, ethnicity, or socio-economic status, we have work to do.

Teaching Compassion?

Finally, a third practice of "transformative education" is compassion. Drawing on the work of Parker Palmer, bell hooks proposes that compassion, or "the capacity for connectedness . . . is at the heart of an ethical life."[43] Rita Nakashima Brock proposes that "good is grounded in our deep awareness of others, our willingness to participate in mutual transformation." It is this deep sense of "connectedness," and the interrelatedness between people, that is at the heart of a "transformative education."[44]

How does one teach compassion? According to Rachel Naomi Remen, compassion *cannot* be taught. She argues that we cannot force or compel people to be compassionate. And yet, compassion may emerge from those moments when people discover that we are connected. Remen offers the following profound thoughts that are equally relevant to teaching divinity or college students as it is to the medical community, whom she addressed in the first instance:

> Compassion emerges from a sense of belonging: the experience that all suffering is like our suffering and all joy is like our joy. When we know ourselves to be connected to all others, acting compassionately is simply the natural thing to do. True compassion requires us to attend to our own humanity, to come to a deep acceptance of our own life as it is. It requires us to come into right relationship with that which is most human in our selves, that which is most capable of suffering.

By recognizing and attending to that basic humanness, our basic human integrity, we find the place of profound connection to all life. That connection then becomes for us the ground of being. It is only through connection that we can recover true compassion, or any authentic sense of meaning in life: a sense of the mysterious, the profound, the sacred nature of the world."[45]

Metaphors of God such as Mourner, Mother, and Midwife portray an image of God that is profoundly relational. This relational, care-giving God becomes manifest when we turn our attention to the other who is more vulnerable and in greater need than ourselves. The care and compassion contained in these divine metaphors encourage us to do the same. In a transformative education, students benefit greatly when given opportunities to discover these connections with the numerous "others" with whom they share this world. Introducing the female divine imagery in the biblical texts, together with theological reflection that is rooted in compassion, will help students to realize that we are all "others" to one another and that we are all worthy of compassion.

TRANSFORMING WORSHIP

By way of conclusion, I want to pay some attention to worship as one space where the process of transformative education may take place. In a place and time where believers gather regularly, one has the opportunity to cultivate practices of remembrance, critical thinking, and compassion. In worship, congregations can imagine the ways in which God's delivering presence comforts and sustains us in times when there seems to be little hope for happy endings or quick fixes. What follows is not an exhaustive treatment of the elements of worship but some suggestions as to how preaching, liturgy, prayers, hymns, and the charge to the congregation may be creatively clothed.

First, *preaching* offers a powerful means of bringing muted and marginalized voices back from oblivion. By telling the stories of mothers, midwives, and wailing women who, throughout the ages, served as embodiments of God's presence, people may learn to think differently about God and to look with new eyes at those who have been forgotten or overlooked in their own communities. For instance, with reference to the story of the midwives Shiphrah and Puah in Exodus 1 (featured in my chapter on God as Midwife), Elizabeth Johnson writes that remembering this story of the brave midwives expands the Exodus story to include the "story of a community of women and men struggling for freedom."[46] Similarly, by delivering sermons on the stories of the female characters who hide somewhere in the midst of the broader story, by allowing their muted voices to speak over microphones to our congregations, we might just start to notice the muted voices in our congregation and in our communities as well: the voices of housekeepers, cashiers, servers, laborers, prostitutes, and homeless wanderers.

Moreover, it is important to preach on the stories of violence in the Bible (e.g., the unspeakable act of violence against the nameless woman in Judges 19, the rape of Dinah in Genesis 34, and the act of incest against Tamar in 2 Samuel 13). Although painful to hear, these stories remind us of the millions of women who suffer rape and abuse every day.[47] These texts of violence can help the congregation to gain insight into the painful, often hushed, reality that is experienced by women near and far in the biblical text as well as in our times. Sermons can move and challenge congregations to find ways to break the cycle of violence and dehumanization.

Regarding the divine metaphors featured in this book, the image of God as Mourner calls on the congregation to lament injustice; the Divine Mother calls on the congregation to protect and care for those in need; and the Divine Midwife calls on the congregation to resist oppression and work for life-giving change.

Second, *liturgy* can provide a powerful means to introduce an alternative understanding of the Deliverer God. For instance, from the wailing woman's call to lament we can learn the importance of creating communal spaces where people can come together to share their grief.[48] Like the wailing women called the community together by raising their voices in weeping and by offering appropriate words and metaphors for the ritual, the contemporary "wailing woman" in the person of the liturgist may join together the community in lament.[49]

South African theologian Denise Ackermann writes compellingly about the need for opportunities for public lament in postapartheid South Africa: "the time is ripe for public liturgical acts in the interest of healing and reconciliation."[50] Even though the Truth and Reconciliation Commission has offered some South Africans the opportunity to confess and to lament (perpetrators of human rights violations were able to confess and to repent, while victims were given a space in which to lament), their mandate was limited and not everyone participated. As a result, Ackermann bemoans the fact that the South African community does not have ongoing public forums of lament. She suggests that religious institutions select liturgies that offer people a space to lament together, to express their pain, anger, and loss, as well as their remorse and repentance in a constructive way.[51]

Excellent examples of the use of litanies in worship come from the work of Elizabeth Johnson, who offers a number of compelling litanies that remember marginal voices, lament injustices, and celebrate resistance. By participating in the responsive reading of the litany, people are actively encouraged to notice and to embrace a different reality. Johnson, for example, cites a litany by Ann Heidkamp [PC(USA)] that celebrates women's power as follows:

> Spirit of Life, we remember the women, named and unnamed, who throughout time have used the gifts you gave them to change the world. We call upon these foremothers to help us discover within ourselves your power—and the ways to use it to bring about the reign of justice and peace.
> We remember Esther and Deborah, whose acts of courage saved their nation . . .
> We remember Mary Magdalene and the other women who followed Jesus . . .
> We remember Phoebe, Priscilla, and the other women leaders of the early church . . .
> We remember the Abbesses of the Middle Ages who kept faith and knowledge alive . . .
> We remember Teresa of Avila and Catherine of Siena, who challenged the corruption of the church during the Renaissance . . .
> We remember our mothers and grandmothers whose lives shaped ours . . .
> And we pray for the women who are victims of violence in their homes . . .
> We pray for those women who face a life of poverty and malnutrition . . .
> We pray for those women who are "firsts" in their fields . . .
> We pray for our daughters and granddaughters . . .[52]

The metaphors featured in this book—which draw on the memories of mothers, midwives, and wailing women throughout the ages in order to embody the delivering presence of God—could well serve as source material for developing new litanies and other liturgical resources. The Seder of Peace proposed by Rabbi Arthur Waskow (cited in the chapter on God as Midwife), for instance, remembers the role of the midwives Shiphrah and Puah as well as of Miriam and Pharaoh's daughter in addition to invoking God as our Midwife.

Prayers offer the opportunity to creatively introduce unconventional metaphors for God, such as Mourner or Wailing Woman, Mother, and Midwife. When we use these female metaphors, which are deeply rooted in tradition, to complement better-known metaphors like Authoritarian Father and Mighty King, we expand our understanding of God. Gradually, these female metaphors work in the minds and hearts of listeners to bring awareness of the relational aspects of God, who is committed to life and love. The necessity of including female metaphors when speaking about God is captured well in Raphael's statement regarding the representation of God in Judaism, which applies to a Christian context as well, "Only where the Jewish God is also called by her female names and pronoun will her voice be heard by all . . . , because a God made exclusively in the masculine image is always calling over women's shoulder to somebody else."[53]

Hymns have a very important role to play in shaping our understanding of God. If we sing only songs that denote powerful images of God (e.g. "Our God Is an Awesome God," "Battle Hymn of the Republic," etc.), we privilege the image of the omnipotent God that resonates with human cravings for power, glory, security, and riches. I would propose that we be deliberate about finding songs that describe God's presence within an anguished creation, the suffering God who works for life in the midst of suffering. In the hymn "God Weeps," God grieves whenever children are abused; wherever women are battered and afraid; wherever there are hungry mouths to feed; and wherever there are creatures dying without cause. Within this hymn there is a sense of the human role in changing these painful situations where people and creation are hurting: "till we change the way we love, God weeps."[54]

In the hymn "Mothering God, You Gave Us Birth," based on Julian of Norwich's visions, mothering metaphors are used to depict the Trinity, offering an alternative to the all-powerful metaphors for God found in many traditional hymns.[55] Brian Wren's lyrics are committed to expanding the image of God by making use of creative metaphors that break through narrow stereotypes. His hymn "Bring Many Names" uses the image of a "strong mother God, working night and day" parallel to a "warm father God, hugging every child."[56]

Finally, the ethical implications embedded in each of these meta-phors for God can be effectively communicated in a *charge to the congregation* to take up their vocation as wailing women, mothers, and midwives to face those suffering from poverty, homelessness, HIV/AIDS, unemployment, illiteracy, disease, hunger, and the many other social problems in our communities and around the world. These female metaphors could go out to all members of the congregation, women as well as men, to challenge them to lament with others and offer care and compassion to each and every person in need. The call to be "midwife" means calling on both men and women to engage in innovative ways and practical projects to relieve the pain and suffering in the world and to bring life into being.

This commitment to the church's mission to serve as God's delivering presence in the world relates to some of the points of a transformative education that I mentioned in the previous section. The worship setting may serve, for example, as a space where connections between people could form. Worship may, for instance, encourage an affluent congregation to act on behalf of people living in extreme poverty. Those who are poor can help the affluent appreciate how the poor also participate in the divine presence as caretakers and life-givers. Audio visual means, photos, personal stories, visits—all may help foster compassion where congregations can truly connect with people in circumstances very different from their own, globally as well as in the cross-cultural setting right around the corner.

Walter Brueggemann once remarked, "The God you speak is the God you get!"[57] It is my hope that in worship, where people come together collectively and individually to cry out to our Deliverer as Mourner, Mother, and Midwife, we shall offer our congregants a theology of presence, rooted in nurturing and preservative love, committed to life for all.

Notes

Chapter 1: Liberating God-Language?

1. Johan Cilliers, *God for Us? An Analysis and Assessment of Dutch Reformed Preaching during the Apartheid Years* (Stellenbosch: Sun Press, 2006), 77.
2. Quoted in Cilliers, *God for Us?* 35–36.
3. It is important to note that that this type of interpretation draws on traditions in the biblical text. South African biblical scholar Ferdinand Deist had good reason to call the Bible (and Deuteronomy in particular) a dangerous book. Deist showed how the Afrikaner community in apartheid South Africa was able to pick up on those biblical traditions that strongly distinguish between "us" and "them," so claiming God for themselves over against the indigenous black people who, to them, represented the heathen Canaanites, from whom Israel had to be kept apart. Biblical prohibitions against Israel mixing with indigenous peoples (e.g. Deut. 7:3–4) as well as the laws forbidding mixing different species and materials (Deut. 22:10–11) provided scriptural support for the South African prohibition against mixed marriages (see Deist, "The Dangers of Deuteronomy: A Page from the Reception History of the Book," in *Studies in Deuteronomy: In Honour of C. J. Labuschagne on the Occasion of His 65th Birthday* (ed. Florentino García Martínez; Leiden: E. J. Brill, 1994), 23.
4. Flora Keshgegian, *Time for Hope: Practices for Living in Today's World* (New York, NY: Continuum, 2006), 11, 53. See also Naim Stifan Ateek, "A Palestine Perspective: The Bible and Liberation," pages 280–86, and Robert Allen Warrior, "A Native American Perspective: Canaanite, Cowboys, and Indians," pages 287–95 in *Voices from the Margin: Interpreting the Bible in the Third World* (ed. R. S. Sugirtharajah; Maryknoll, NY: Orbis Books, 1991).
5. Catherine Keller, "The Love of Postcolonialism: Theology in the Interstices of Empire," in *Postcolonial Theologies: Divinity and Empire* (eds. Catherine Keller et al.; St. Louis, MS: Chalice Press, 2004), 222. See also Elisabeth Schüssler

Fiorenza, *The Power of the Word: Scripture and the Rhetoric of Empire* (Minneapolis, MN: Fortress Press, 2007).

6. Catherine Keller, "Preemption and Omnipotence: A Niebuhrian Prophecy," in *God and Power: Counter-Apocalyptic Journeys* (Minneapolis, MN: Fortress Press, 2005), 17–34. See also the "Liberty Bible" and a "God Bless America" cross covered in the Star-Spangled Banner for sale on the Internet that demonstrate the reality of a "God-for-us" theology, which assumes a conflation between God and Nation.

7. Keller, "Preemption and Omnipotence," 29–30.

8. Rita Nakashima Brock, "A New Thing in the Land: The Female Surrounds the Warrior," in *Power, Powerlessness, and the Divine: New Inquiries in Bible and Theology* (ed. Cynthia L. Rigby; Atlanta, GA: Scholars Press, 1997), 140.

9. Susan Ackerman, *Warrior, Dancer, Seductress, Queen: Women in Judges and Biblical Israel* (Anchor Bible Reference Library; New York, NY: Doubleday, 2002), 32–38. See Ackerman's exposition of the way Judg. 5:4–5 and Judg. 5:6–7 form a poetic diptych in which God's action and Deborah's action are paired—"Israel's holy war as a cosmic activity" being executed in "the earthly context of the battle," 36.

10. Quoted in Judith Butler, *Gender Trouble: Feminism and the Subversion of Identity* (New York, NY: Routledge, 1990), 1–6.

11. Susan Niditch, "Eroticism and Death in the Tale of Jael," in *Women in the Hebrew Bible* (ed. Alice Bach; New York, NY: Routledge, 1999), 307; Gale A. Yee, "By the Hand of a Woman: The Metaphor of the Woman Warrior in Judges 4," *Semeia* 61 (1993): 116–25.

12. Musa Dube, "Jumping the Fire with Judith: Postcolonial Feminist Hermeneutics of Liberation," in *Feminist Interpretation of the Bible and the Hermeneutics of Liberation* (ed. Silvia Schroer and Sophia Bietenhard; London: Sheffield Academic Press, 2003), 60–74.

13. In her analysis of various interpretations of this intriguing image of the woman warrior, Yee notes that some feminists reject human as well as divine women warrior images as liberating images for women today ("By the Hand of a Woman," 106). See in particular the article by Carol Christ, "Feminist Liberation Theology and Yahweh as Holy Warrior: An Analysis of Symbol," in *Women's Spirit Bonding* (ed. Janet Kalven and Mary I. Buckley; New York, NY: Pilgrim Press, 1984), 202–12.

14. See http://youtu.be/1aZdAyHVjzQ.

15. Ackerman, *Warrior, Dancer, Seductress, Queen*, 28.

16. Deborah Sawyer, *God, Gender, and the Bible* (New York, NY: Routledge, 2002), 70.

17. Keshgegian rightly notes that many people worldwide are still struggling with trauma—if not firsthand, then at least with the effects of second-hand trauma; that is, trauma that has passed on through generations (*Time for Hope*, 98).

18. In this regard, it is significant that, as Andrea Fröchtling notes in her study *Exiled God and Exiled Peoples: Memoria Passionis and the Perception of God during and after Apartheid and Shoah* (Ökumenische Studien 22; Berlin-Hamburg-Münster: LIT Verlag, 2002), the forced removals in both apartheid South Africa and Nazi Germany during the Holocaust (Shoah) were experienced by the victims as "rupture" according to which "individual and communal life-stories" were

experienced as completely ruptured and/or interrupted, 3–4. As one South African interviewee of Fröchtling recalls, she was unable to talk to or about God in the same way she had done before she had suffered trauma at the hands of the apartheid regime. She explained, "And then you have to find new words to talk to God, because the old words, they don't work any longer," 120.

19. James C. Scott, *Domination and the Art of Resistance: Hidden Transcripts* (New Haven, CT: Yale University Press, 1992), 4ff. Walter Brueggemann draws on Scott's notion of "hidden transcripts" in order to suggest that "in oppressed peasant communities the peasants maintain a 'hidden transcript,' a coded account of reality that is not public or known by the overlords, an account that tells the truth about social reality and that regularly subverts the pretentious posturing and oppressive policies of the powerful. The hidden transcript empowers the vulnerable in a way that may eventually defeat the false script of the overlords"—"Alien Witness: How God's People Challenge Empire," *Christian Century* (March 6, 2007): 28, 31.

20. Jacqueline E. Lapsley, *Whispering the Word: Hearing Women's Stories in the Old Testament* (Louisville, KY: Westminster John Knox Press, 2005), 18.

21. Gina Hens-Piazza, *Nameless, Blameless, and Without Shame: Two Cannibal Mothers before a King* (Collegeville, MN: Liturgical Press, 2003), 83–84.

22. Hens-Piazza, *Nameless*, 94.

23. Catherine Keller, "Ms. Calculating the Endtimes: Gender Styles of Apocalypse," *God and Power: Counter-Apocalyptic Journeys* (Minneapolis, MN: Fortress Press, 2005), 57.

24. See Rainer Albertz, *Israel in Exile: The History and Literature of the Sixth Century BCE* (trans. David Green; Atlanta, GA: Society of Biblical Literature, 2003).

25. Daniel L. Smith-Christopher, *A Biblical Theology of Exile* (Overtures to Biblical Theology; Minneapolis, MN: Fortress Press, 2001), 106–7.

26. In his book *Reading the Hebrew Bible after the Shoah* (Minneapolis, MN: Fortress Press, 2008), Marvin Sweeney shows how various parts of the Hebrew Bible attempt to make sense of issues regarding God's involvement in the cataclysmic events of the destruction of Jerusalem and the Babylonian exile. It is important to see how the various writers of the biblical books shared the same questions—questions that we are still asking thousands of years later, regarding the Shoah as well as other situations of extreme suffering, 166.

27. Sweeney, *Reading the Hebrew Bible after the Shoah*, 155, 228–29.

28. Catherine Keller, "The Armageddon of 9/11: Lament for the New Millennium," *God and Power: Counter-Apocalyptic Journeys* (Minneapolis, MN: Fortress Press, 2005), 10.

29. Smith-Christopher, *Biblical Theology of Exile*, 107.

30. Edward Said, "Reflections on Exile," in *Reflections on Exile and Other Essays* (Cambridge, MA: Harvard University Press, 2000), 178.

31. Smith-Christopher, *Biblical Theology of Exile*, 107.

32. Robert P. Carroll, "The Myth of the Empty Land," *Semeia* 59 (1992): 79–93.

33. Gayatri Chakravorty Spivak, "Can the Subaltern Speak?" in *Marxism and the Interpretation of Culture* (ed. Cary Nelson and Lawrence Grossberg; London: Macmillan, 1988), 28.

Chapter 2: God as Mourner

1. To "keen" is to weep or wail and is derived from the Old Irish word *caoinim*. "Keen" came into English usage as an adjective meaning "sharp, like the keen edge of a knife, or something that is highly sensitive, intense, or piercing." Thus, a "keener" is someone who weeps, mourns, or laments with an intensity that moves others to expressions of grief. For the purposes of this book, "keeners," "mourning women" and "wailing women" will be used interchangeably.

2. Sue Monk Kidd, *The Secret Life of Bees* (Second Edition; New York: Penguin Books, 2003); Gina Prince-Bythewood. 2008. *The Secret Life of Bees*. Film. Directed by Gina Prince-Bythewood. Los Angeles, CA: Fox Searchlight Pictures.

3. Sue Monk Kid, *The Secret Life of Bees*, 120.

4. http://philosophermoms.blogspot.com/2009_04_01_archive.html.   Accessed March 26, 2011.

5. Denise Ackermann, "On Hearing and Lamenting: Faith and Truth-Telling," in *To Remember and to Heal: Theological and Psychological Reflections on Truth and Reconciliation* (ed. H. Russel Botman and Robin M. Petersen; Cape Town: Human and Rousseau Uitgewers, 1996), 53.

6. Flora Keshgegian, *Time for Hope: Practices for Living in Today's World* (New York, NY: Continuum, 2006), 100.

7. Louis Stulman, *Order amid Chaos: Jeremiah as Symbolic Tapestry* (Sheffield: Sheffield Academic Press, 1998), 174.

8. According to Kathleen O'Connor, the book Jeremiah seeks for "language to name this world of catastrophe and misery." She says, "Its wide collection of poems, stories, and sermons over and over again depicts a shattered world, usually in symbolic form." "Rekindling Life, Igniting Hope," *Journal for Preachers* 30/2 (Lent 2007): 30.

9. Kathleen M. O'Connor, "The Tears of God and Divine Character in Jeremiah 2–9," in *God in the Fray: A Tribute to Walter Brueggemann* (ed. Tod Linafelt and Timothy K. Beal; Minneapolis, MN: Fortress Press, 1998), 173–79.

10. See, e.g., Renita Weems, *Battered Love: Marriage, Sex, and Violence in the Hebrew Prophets* (OBT; Minneapolis, MN: Fortress Press, 1995); Gale Yee, *Poor Banished Children of Eve: Woman as Evil in the Hebrew Bible* (Minneapolis, MN: Augsburg Fortress Press, 2003), 81–134. For a summary of the various interpretative strategies followed by feminist interpreters regarding these problematic metaphors, see the chapter on the feminist theological response to the prophets in Julia O'Brien, *Challenging Prophetic Metaphor: Theology and Ideology in the Prophets* (Louisville, KY: Westminster John Knox Press, 2008), 29–48.

11. See also David R. Blumenthal, *Facing the Abusing God: A Theology of Protest* (Louisville, KY: Westminster John Knox Press, 1993).

12. Zachary Braiterman's book *(God) after Auschwitz: Tradition and Change in Post-Holocaust Jewish Thought* is a good example of this struggle to see whether belief in God is still possible after what people have seen in the extermination camps (Princeton, NJ: Princeton University Press, 1998). Compare also Richard Rubenstein's famous words, "When I say we live in the time of the death of God, I mean that the thread uniting God and man, heaven and earth, has been broken. We stand in a cold, silent, unfeeling cosmos, unaided by any purposeful power beyond our own resources. After Auschwitz, what else can a

Jew say about God?" in Rubenstein, *After Auschwitz: Radical Theology and Contemporary Judaism* (Indianapolis, IN: Bobbs-Merrill, 1966), 151–52.

13. Walter Brueggemann, *To Pluck Up, to Tear Down: A Commentary on the Book of Jeremiah 1–25* (ITC; Grand Rapids, MI: Wm. B. Eerdmans Publishing Co., 1988), 88. For a contrasting view, see Jack R. Lundbom, *Jeremiah 1–20* (AB 21A; New York, NY: Doubleday, 1999), 535–37.

14. O'Connor, "Tears of God," 180–81.

15. Rabbi Kalonymus Kalman Shapiro, quoted in Herbert J. Levine, *Sing unto God a New Song: A Contemporary Reading of the Psalms* (Bloomington, IN: Indiana University Press, 1995), 219. For an insightful essay on the range of rabbinic interpretations that feature various variations of God's tears, see Herbert W. Basser, "A Love for All Seasons: Weeping in Jewish Sources," in *Holy Tears: Weeping in the Religious Imagination* (ed. Kimberley Christine Patton and John Stratton Hawley; Princeton, NJ: Princeton University Press, 2005), 178–200.

16. Basser, "Love for All Seasons," 188.

17. Levine, *Sing unto God*, 196.

18. O'Connor, "Tears of God," 184. Stulman also uses a type of "rupturing" language to describe the role of pathos in creating alternative theological imagery: "Thus we witness the shattering of God and the shattering of Jeremiah both of which contribute to the wild, jumbled, and pathos-filled world of the text," *Order amid Chaos*, 186.

19. O'Connor, "Tears of God," 185. O'Connor concludes her essay by saying, "Without such disjunction in the divine character, healing would not be possible." See also Kimberley Christine Patton and John Stratton Hawley, who argue that weeping has an "efficacious, or even theurgic role" as it is able to "evoke divine response, especially that of compassion or mercy, where none had previously been forthcoming"—"Introduction," in *Holy Tears: Weeping in the Religious Imagination* (ed. Kimberley Christine Patton and John Stratton Hawley; Princeton, NJ: Princeton University Press, 2005), 2.

20. O'Connor, "Tears of God," 181–82.

21. Nicholas Wolterstorff, "The Wounds of God: Calvin's Theology of Social Justice," *The Reformed Journal* 37/6 (1987): 16.

22. Terence E. Fretheim, who has been strongly influenced by the theology of pathos put forth by Abraham Heschel, argues that God is not indifferent to what happens to people. Rather, God enters into mourning, suggesting that this mourning is not the end, but that God is at work in the midst of situations of death and destruction to bring forth life, *The Suffering of God* (Overtures to Biblical Theology; Minneapolis, MN: Fortress Press, 1984), 136.

23. Levine, *Sing unto God*, 196.

24. Kimberley Christine Patton and John Stratton point out that it is noteworthy how often "public, collective, ritual lamentation is assigned to women"—especially with regard to "funerary weeping." They refer to instances of this not only in ancient Japan, Greece, and Mexico but also in modern-day India, Greece, and Iran, "Introduction," 12; Tom Lutz, *Crying: The Natural and Cultural History of Tears* (New York, NY: W. W. Norton and Co., 1999), 222–23.

25. In addition to crying aloud, some women played flutes to mimic the piercing sounds of wailing. Compare, e.g., the "flute-players" and people "making a

commotion" who surrounded the home of a young girl who had just died
(Matt. 9:23; Mark 5:38–39; Luke 8:52).

26. Fokkelien van Dijk-Hemmes, "Traces of Women's Texts in the Hebrew
Bible," *On Gendering Texts: Female and Male Voices in the Hebrew Bible* (ed. Athalya
Brenner and Fokkelien van Dijk-Hemmes; Biblical Interpretation Series 1.
Leiden: Brill, 1993), 84. For an exposition of the role of the Egyptian mythical
wailing women Isis and Nephthys in the cult of Osiris, see Claas Jouco
Bleeker's essay "Isis and Nephthys as Wailing Women," *Numen* 5 (1958): 1–17.

27. Van Dijk-Hemmes, "Traces of Women's Texts," 84. As Athalya Brenner,
argues, "Women who took up mourning as a vocation had to learn the
formulae of their trade," *The Israelite Woman: Social Role and Literary Type in
Biblical Narrative* (Sheffield: JSOT, 1985), 37. See also the existence of
professional female lamenters in Sumer that are connected to the goddess
Ningal lamenting over the Sumerian city of Ur, in S. D. Goitein, "Women as
Creators of Biblical Genres," *Prooftexts* 8/1 (1988): 26.

28. Van Dijk-Hemmes, "Traces of Women's Texts," 84.

29. Goitein, "Women as Creators," 26.

30. Tova Gamliel, "'Wailing Lore' in Yemenite–Israeli Community: Bereavement,
Expertise, and Therapy," *Social Science and Medicine*, 65/7 (2007): 1501–11. Available
online at http://www.sciencedirect.com/science. Accessed October 6, 2008.

31. Kathleen Sands, "Tragedy, Theology, and Feminism in the Time after Time,"
New Literary History 35/1 (2004): 43.

32. Keshgegian, *Time for Hope*, 113.

33. In his fascinating book on a natural and cultural history of tears, Tom Lutz
analyzes this ability of tears to change the environment in which the one who
cries finds him- or herself. The act of crying constitutes a refusal to accept the
present reality as it is. In this regard, Lutz draws on Jean Paul Sartre's
description of tears as the "magical transformation" of the world, in which the
subject, through his or her tears, changes his or her relation to the world.
However, this internal effect also has an external purpose: through his or her
tears, the subject consciously or unconsciously attempts to change the attitude
of the person/group at whom the tears are directed, *Crying*, 225, 226, 240.

34. Goitein, "Women as Creators," 27.

35. Shoshana Felman, "Education and Crisis," in *Trauma: Explorations in Memory*
(ed. Cathy Caruth; Baltimore, MD: John Hopkins University Press, 1995), 15.

36. Felman, "Education and Crisis," 47.

37. Felman, "Education and Crisis," 16. Felman quotes Camus as he relates the
role of the physician: "Dr Rieux resolved to compile his chronicle, so that he
should not be one of those who hold their peace but should bear witness in
favour of those plague-stricken people, so that some memorial of the injustice
done them might endure."

38. Flora Keshgegian notes that "the temptation to 'forget' is ever present. Yet
always at the heart of the process is the call to remember in order to remember
one's life," *Redeeming Memories: A Theology of Healing and Transformation*
(Nashville, TN: Abingdon Press, 2000), 36.

39. Goitein, "Women as Creators," 3.

40. Goitein, "Women as Creators," 2.

41. Pamela J. Scalise argues that the "the messenger formula, 'thus says the Lord,'

indicates the prophetic use of the dirge genre in this context"—"The Way of Weeping: Reading the Path of Grief in Jeremiah," *Word and World* 22/4 (2002): 417.

42. Terence Fretheim, *Jeremiah* (Smyth and Helwys Bible Commentary; Macon, GA: Smyth and Helwys, 2002), 159.

43. Lundbom shows how the catchwords "weeping" and "I might weep" in this poem connect 9:10 [MT 9:9] backward to 9:1 [MT 8:23], as well as forward with 9:17–19 [MT 16–18] and 9:20 [MT 19] by means of the catchwords "lament . . . dirge"; "dirge singers . . . lament . . . lament" and "lament . . . dirge." Even though Lundbom strongly asserts that the speaker in 9:1 [MT 8:23] and 9:10–11 [MT 9–10] is Jeremiah and not God, his arguments may actually be used to bring into sharper focus the link between the divine tears and the community's response, *Jeremiah 1–20*, 549.

44. With regard to childhood sexual abuse, Flora Keshgegian, drawing on the work of Judith Herman, notes that to immerse oneself in the painful memories of the traumatic event is at the same time "the most necessary and the most dreaded task of this stage of recovery," *Redeeming Memories*, 41.

45. O'Connor, "Rekindling Life, Igniting Hope," 31. See also Kathleen O'Connor, "A Family Comes Undone," *Review and Expositor* 105/2 (2008): 201–12.

46. Flora Keshgegian describes the recovery process as follows: "This process heeds the imperative to honor the dead and to remember suffering, by recognizing the persistence of an unhealed wound, and yet responds to the yearning for life . . . It faces the deaths and losses without avoidance, yet makes possible new and renewed connections in life," *Redeeming Memories*, 43, 88.

47. Keshgegian, *Redeeming Memories*, 23. Keshgegian quotes Adrienne Rich's poem, "Natural Resources," in *The Dream of a Common Language: Poems 1974–1977* (W. W. Norton 1993), 60.

48. Tova Gamliel, "Performance Versus Social Invisibility: What Can Be Learned from the Wailing Culture of Old-Age Yemenite-Jewish Women?" *Women Studies International Forum* 31/3 (May–June 2008), 209–18 (p. 216). Available online at http://www.sciencedirect.com/science. Accessed October 6, 2008.

49. Keshgegian, *Redeeming Memories*, 155.

50. Stulman, *Order amid Chaos*, 160.

51. Stulman, *Order amid Chaos*, 187.

52. For more information on this well-documented phenomenon, see the series of studies cited in Gamliel, "Wailing Lore," 1503.

53. Gamliel observes that the office of the wailing woman was most often associated with older women. It seems that a woman who had seen something of life, who perhaps had experienced loss herself, was deemed qualified to lead the community in wailing, "Performance Versus Social Invisibility," 212.

54. Kimberley Christine Patton and John Stratton Hawley, "Introduction," 14.

55. See also Kathleen D. L. Billman and Daniel Migliore's book, which bears the name of Rachel, on the recovery of lament in the church, *Rachel's Cry: Prayer of Lament and Rebirth of Hope* (Cleveland, OH: United Church Press, 1999).

56. As O'Connor formulates this perspective, "In Jeremiah, God's tears are more powerful even than the armies under divine command because, for a poetic moment at least, God, people, and cosmos articulate a common suffering and God changes sides"—"Tears of God," 18.

57. See Jürgen Moltmann's seminal work, *The Crucified God: The Cross of Christ as the*

Foundation and Criticism of Christian Theology (New York, NY: Harper and Row, 1974).

58. Nicholas Wolterstorff, *Lament for a Son* (Grand Rapids, MI: Wm. B. Eerdmans Publishing Co., 1987), 26.

59. O'Connor, "Tears of God," 184.

60. Wolterstorff, "The Wounds of God," 22.

61. Wolterstorff, "The Wounds of God," 16–17.

62. Denise Ackermann, "On Hearing and Lamenting," 54.

63. Ackermann, "On Hearing and Lamenting," 54–55.

64. O'Connor, "Tears of God," 184.

65. Chuan-Seng Song, *The Tears of Lady Meng: A Parable of People's Political Theology* (Maryknoll, NY: Orbis Books, 1981), 44.

66. Composed by Dan Heymann and published by Muffled Music (administered by Kobalt Music/Sheer Music) and Geoff Paynter Music Publishing. Online at http://www.weeping.info/Weeping-lyrics.html. Accessed May 16, 2011.

67. http://www.weeping.info/Weeping.html. Accessed May 16, 2011. It is interesting to note that in one of the various manifestations of this song, the lyrics of the Afrikaans version have been transformed to denote the painful reality of poverty in South Africa that has to be resisted by means of tears.

68. This particular rendition of "Weeping" appears on the Soweto String Quartet's CD *Renaissance*. Visit http://www.sowetostringquartet.co.za/albums.aspx for more details.

69. See Levine's comment, "Israel had no physical means to exact its desired revenge for such psychic violence; its only weapon was words," *Sing unto God*, 185–86.

70. David G. Garber, "Facing Traumatizing Texts: Reading Nahum's Nationalistic Rage," *Review and Expositor*, 105/2 (2008): 292.

71. Keshgegian, *Redeeming Memories*, 68.

72. Quoted in Pumla Gobodo-Madikizela, *A Human Being Died That Night: A South African Woman Confronts the Legacy of Apartheid* (Boston, MA: Houghton Mifflin Co., 2003), 14–15.

73. Gobodo-Madikizela, *Human Being*, 127–28.

74. Scalise, "The Way of Weeping," 422.

75. Walter Brueggemann, "Faith at the *Nullpunkt*," in *The End of the World and the Ends of God: Science and Theology on Eschatology* (ed. John Polkinghorne and Michael Welker; Harrisburg, PA: Trinity, 2000), 143–54.

76. Keshgegian, *Redeeming Memories*, 76.

Chapter 3: God as Mother

1. The focus on nurturing mothers in no way suggests that fathers are not a nurturing presence in their children's lives. I am reminded of the example of Sara Ruddick, who calls her husband her "co-mother." Ruddick's book, *Maternal Thinking: Toward a Politics of Peace*, accordingly works with a broad definition of mothering, maintaining that both men and women are qualified to "mother" (New York, NY: Ballantine Books, 1989), 40–51.

2. Erika Langmuir, *Imagining Childhood* (New Haven, CT: Yale University Press), 39.

3. Melissa Raphael, *The Female Face of God in Auschwitz: A Jewish Feminist Theology of the Holocaust* (Religion and Gender; London: Routledge, 2003), 10.

4. The effects of trauma are long lasting. Flora Keshgegian argues: "if the injuries are not attended to, if the trauma is hidden and not recognized, the wounds fester." And even though "time heals all wounds," the scars remain forever, *Time for Hope: Practices for Living in Today's World* (New York, NY: Continuum, 2006), 100.

5. Ann Johnston, "A Prophetic Vision of an Alternative Community: A Reading of Isaiah 40–55," in *Uncovering Ancient Stones: Essays in Memory of H. Neil Richardson* (ed. Lewis M. Hopfe; Winona Lake, ID: Eisenbrauns, 1994), 32.

6. Paul D. Hanson, "Divine Power in Powerlessness," in *Power, Powerlessness, and the Divine: New Inquiries in Bible and Theology* (ed. Cynthia L. Rigby; Atlanta, GA: Scholars Press, 1997), 179–80.

7. The Hebrew for this phrase is φο4λε4δα4η, which is the participle form of the verb "to bear"; literally meaning "the one who bears." I will be translating "mother in labor" instead of "woman in labor," based on the notion that "mothering" does begin after the child is born but already exists in the nine months before the act of giving birth.

8. Sarah J. Dille, *Mixing Metaphors: God as Mother and Father in Deutero-Isaiah* (JSOT Sup. 398; Gender, Culture, Theory, 13; London: T & T Clark International, 2004), 116–17.

9. The structuring metaphor of Isa. 49:13–50:3, 51:12–52:10, and 54:1–17 is the Divine Husband who is first accused of abandoning his wife and subsequently seeks reconciliation, Dille, *Mixing Metaphors*, 139. See also Kathleen M. O'Connor, "'Speak Tenderly to Jerusalem:' Second Isaiah's Reception and Use of Daughter Zion," *Princeton Seminary Bulletin* 20 (1999): 289–92.

10. Mayer I. Gruber, "The Motherhood of God in Second Isaiah," *Revue Biblique* 90 (1983): 358.

11. John J. Schmitt, "The Motherhood of God and Zion as Mother," *Revue Biblique* 92 (1985): 563, 569.

12. Rainer Albertz, *Die Exilszeit* (Biblische Enzyklopädie 7; Stuttgart: Kohlhammer Verlag, 2001), 115; *Persönlikche Frömmigkeit und offizielle Religion* (Stuttgart: Calwer Verlag, 1978), 178–80.

13. See also Leila Leah Bronner's argument that, in light of the chaos people were experiencing during the time of the exile, the prophet drew on nurturing imagery from the realm of the family and, accordingly, female experience that constituted the only form of security for an exilic people, "Gynomorphic Imagery in Exilic Isaiah 40–66," *Dor le Dor* 12 (1983–1984): 82.

14. Joseph Blenkinsopp, "Second Isaiah—Prophet of Universalism." *JSOT* 41 (1988): 84.

15. The identity of the servant in the servant songs has long been the subject of various debates. Some scholars argue that the servant is an individual—the Messiah—who represents the ideal Israel, the exilic community. The individual may be the prophet himself or, in the case of the first servant song (Isa. 42:1–7), Cyrus, the Persian emperor. See Blenkinsopp, "Second Isaiah," 89. An alternative proposal is that the servant in the first song refers to Israel; i.e., a broken people who shall not break but who, through God's power, will fulfill

their original calling—the promise once made to Abraham—to serve as a blessing to the nations. See Walter Brueggemann, *Isaiah 40–66* (WBC; Louisville, KY: Westminster John Knox Press, 1998), 42.

16. Blenkinsopp, "Second Isaiah," 85, 88.

17. Edward Said, "Reflections on Exile," in *Reflections on Exile and Other Essays* (Cambridge, MA: Harvard University Press, 2000), 177.

18. Blenkinsopp, "Second Isaiah," 91. See also Samuel E. Balentine, "The Politics of Religion in the Persian Period," in *After the Exile: Essays in Honour of Rex Mason* (ed. John Barton and David J. Reimer; Macon, GA: Mercer University Press, 1996), 137–39.

19. Blenkinsopp, "Second Isaiah," 90–91.

20. Walter Brueggemann, "Alien Witness: How God's People Challenge Empire," *Christian Century* (March 6, 2007): 28, 31.

21. The focus on female imagery in the context of Deutero-Isaiah does not preclude the fact that the Bible also contains compassionate, nonviolent male images. However, the predominance of the female imagery in this particular literary context is worth exploring.

22. Said, "Reflections on Exile," 174.

23. Flora Keshgegian, *Redeeming Memories: A Theology of Healing and Transformation* (Nashville, TN: Abingdon Press, 2000), 64.

24. James Muilenburg has introduced the provocative designation, "the birthpangs of God," arguing that this metaphor signifies that God is bringing a new creation into the world. See Muilenburg, "The Book of Isaiah," in *The Interpreter's Bible* (Nashville, TN: Abingdon Press, 1956), 5:473. Phyllis Trible develops this argument further in *God and the Rhetoric of Sexuality* (Overtures to Biblical Theology; Philadelphia, PA: Fortress Press, 1978), 64.

25. Fokkelien van Dijk-Hemmes, "Traces of Women's Texts in the Hebrew Bible," in *On Gendering Texts: Female and Male Voices in the Hebrew Bible* (ed. Athalya Brenner and Fokkelien van Dijk-Hemmes; Biblical Interpretation Series 1. Leiden: Brill, 1993), 94.

26. Walter Brueggemann interprets the imagery in v. 15 to denote a victory march, thus giving precedence to the warrior image that is used for God, *Isaiah 40–66*, 47. In contrast, Paul D. Hanson argues that God is removing the obstacles before the returning exiles as a sign of God's new creation, *Isaiah 40–66* (Interpretation; Louisville, KY: Westminster John Knox Press, 1995), 52. I argue that Hanson's understanding better takes into account the presence of the metaphor of a mother in labor.

27. Dille argues that that the metaphors of God as Artisan and God as Father/Mother that interanimate creatively should be read in terms of the strong anti-idol discourse (Isa. 44) that precedes this text. It seems that, in Isaiah 45, the prophet argues against the Babylonian artisans who fashion idols, and shows that *God* is the creator of God's servants—Israel and Cyrus— *Mixing Metaphors,* 107–15.

28. With reference to Isaiah 49, Patricia Tull Willey argues that this portrayal of God's comfort in terms of a mother's love is a response to earlier imagery in Lamentations and Jeremiah. Patricia Tull Willey, *Remember the Former Things: The Recollection of Previous Texts in Second Isaiah* (Atlanta, GA: Scholars Press, 1997), 157, 188–91.

29. Willey, *Remember the Former Things*, 267. See also O'Connor, "'Speak Tenderly to Jerusalem,'" 281–94.

30. Willem A. M. Beuken, "The Main Theme of Trito-Isaiah: 'The Servants of YHWH,'" *JSOT* 47 (1990): 83–84.

31. For the role of the metaphor of nursing as an image of restoration, see L. Juliana M. Claassens, *The God who Provides: Biblical Images of Divine Nourishment* (Nashville, TN: Abingdon Press, 2004), 80–82.

32. Dille illustrates how disruptive the exile was regarding family life, calling to mind examples of mothers separated from their children. The breakdown in the mother/child relationship is most painfully illustrated in the book of Lamentations, *Mixing Metaphors*, 144–45.

33. Catherine Keller, "Preemption and Omnipotence: A Niebuhrian Prophecy," *God and Power: Counter-Apocalyptic Journeys* (Minneapolis, MN: Fortress Press, 2005), 29.

34. In a May 2003 speech on board the *USS Lincoln*, during which George W. Bush declared an end to major combat in Iraq—and, incidentally, cited one of the texts featured in this chapter (Isa. 42:7)—the president exclaimed, "From distant bases or ships at sea, we sent planes and missiles that could destroy an enemy division or strike a single bunker. Marines and soldiers charged to Baghdad across 350 miles of hostile ground in one of the swiftest advances of heavy arms in history. You have shown the world the skill and the might of the American armed forces." Online at http://www.cnn.com/2003/US/05/01/bush.transcript/. Accessed October 27, 2008.

35. Rita Nakashima Brock, "A New Thing in the Land: The Female Surrounds the Warrior," in *Power, Powerlessness, and the Divine: New Inquiries in Bible and Theology* (ed. Cynthia L. Rigby; Atlanta, GA: Scholars Press, 1997), 158.

36. Brock, "A New Thing," 158.

37. Katheryn Pfisterer Darr has argued that the "travailing woman simile" in v. 40 should be understood in light of its juxtaposition with the warrior image. The "travailing woman simile" is regularly used in biblical texts (such as Isa. 13:6–8; 21:1–11; Jer. 6:23–24; Ps. 48:5–6) to describe people's feelings of helplessness and despair in the face of enemy attacks. However, by aligning it with the warrior metaphor in the preceding verse, Darr argues, Deutero-Isaiah reshapes the metaphor of a mother in labor: This juxtaposition transforms the conventional meaning of the travailing woman metaphor so that it does not describe panic or fear, but rather God's powerful ability to act, which stands in contrast to the powerlessness of the people, "Like Warrior, like Woman: Destruction and Deliverance in Isaiah 42:10–17," *CBQ* 49 (1987): 564–65 and "Two Unifying Female Images in the Book of Isaiah," in *Uncovering Ancient Stones: Essays in Memory of H. Niel Richardson* (ed. Lewis M. Hopfe; Winona Lake, ID: Eisenbrauns, 1994), 25, 27.

38. See, e.g., the work by Renita Weems, *Battered Love: Marriage, Sex, and Violence in the Hebrew Prophets* (OBT; Minneapolis, MN: Fortress Press, 1995).

39. See David J. A. Clines, *I, He, We, They: A Literary Approach to Isaiah 53* (JSOT Sup.1; Sheffield: JSOT, 1976).

40. Kathleen O'Connor, "Rekindling Life, Igniting Hope," *Journal for Preachers* 30/2 (Lent 2007): 34.

41. The subtitle of Ruddick's book, *Maternal Thinking: Toward a Politics of Peace* is

suggestive of the fact that "the effort of world protection may come to seem a 'natural' extension of maternal work," 57, 81.

42. Johnston, "A Prophetic Vision," 37–38. See also Hanson, "Divine Power," 186.

43. Brueggemann, *Isaiah 40–66*, 82.

44. Blenkinsopp points out that there is a certain ambiguity in the exilic community's perception of the Gentile world and their relations with the nations, "Second Isaiah," 89. See also Joel Kaminsky, *"Yet I Loved Jacob": Reclaiming the Biblical Concept of Election* (Nashville, TN: Abingdon Press, 2007), 140–46.

45. Ruddick, *Maternal Thinking*, 72.

46. Ruddick, *Maternal Thinking*, 30, 68.

47. Paul Hanson, *The People Called: The Growth of Community in the Bible* (San Francisco, CA: Harper and Row, 1987), 467.

48. Catherine Keller, "The Love Supplement: Christianity and Empire," in *God and Power: Counter-Apocalyptic Journeys* (Minneapolis, MN: Fortress Press, 2005), 116.

49. Gayatri Chakravorty Spivak, *A Critique of Postcolonial Reason: Toward a History of the Vanishing Present* (Cambridge, MA: Harvard University Press, 1999), 383.

50. Spivak, *Critique of Postcolonial Reason*, 383.

51. Keller, "The Love Supplement," 132–33.

52. Keller, "Preemption and Omnipotence," 30.

53. Hanson, *The People Called*, 244.

54. Robert Gibbs, *Why Ethics? Signs of Responsibility* (Princeton, NJ: Princeton University Press, 2000), 106.

Chapter 4: God as Midwife

1. Sophia Chirongoma, "Women, Poverty, and HIV in Zimbabwe: An Exploration of Inequalities in Health Care," in *Africa Women, Religion, and Health: Essays in Honor of Mercy Amba Ewudziwa Oduyoye* (ed. Isabel Phiri and Sarojini Nadar; Pietermaritzburg: Cluster Publications, 2000), 177.

2. Tal Ilan, *Jewish Women in Greco-Roman Palestine* (Peabody, MA: Hendrickson, 1996), 189. The profession of midwife is typically associated with females. In rabbinic literature, only feminine forms are used to denote it, suggesting that in Palestine and in the Greco-Roman period this profession most likely was limited to women.

3. Barbara Ehrenreich and Deirdre English document the ways in which, over the centuries, the vital role of midwives has been subject to suspicion and opposition from the emerging male-dominated medical profession, in *Witches, Midwives, and Nurses: A History of Women Healers* (New York, NY: Feminist Press, 1973).

4. Elaine Wainwright, *Women Healing/Healing Women: The Genderization of Healing in Early Christianity* (London: Equinox Publishing, 2006), 40. This connection is poignantly expressed in a painting by Sheva Chaya titled *Midwife*. See Sheva Chaya's Website for an image of the painting: http://shevachaya.com/gallery.php?categoryid=2&category=Women's Expression. Accessed March 26, 2011.

5. Wainwright, *Women Healing/Healing Women*, 40–41.

6. Although the psalmist most likely was a man, at times I will use the female pronoun in order to encourage imagining a female subject.

7. Marvin E. Tate, *Psalms 51-100* (WBC; Dallas, TX: Word Books, 1990), 212–13.

8. James Luther Mays, *Psalms* (Interpretation; Louisville, KY: John Knox Press, 1994), 17, 19.

9. Samuel E. Balentine, "The Politics of Religion in the Persian Period," in *After the Exile: Essays in Honour of Rex Mason* (eds. John Barton and David J. Reimer; Macon, GA: Mercer University Press, 1996), 129–30.

10. Karen Baker-Fletcher, *Dancing with God: The Trinity from a Womanist Perspective* (St. Louis, MS: Chalice Press, 2007), 112. See also Flora Keshgegian, *Time for Hope: Practices for Living in Today's World* (New York, NY: Continuum, 2006), 5.

11. Balentine, "Politics of Religion," 129–30.

12. Flora A. Keshgegian, *Redeeming Memories: A Theology of Healing and Transformation* (Nashville, TN: Abingdon Press, 2000), 28–29.

13. Keshgegian, *Redeeming Memories,* 43.

14. Herbert J. Levine, *Sing unto God a New Song: A Contemporary Reading of the Psalms* (Bloomington, IN: Indiana University Press, 1995), 178–79.

15. Jacqueline E. Lapsley, *Whispering the Word: Hearing Women's Stories in the Old Testament* (Louisville, KY: Westminster John Knox Press, 2005), 18.

16. The identity of Shiphrah and Puah is ambiguous. They could have been either *Hebrew midwives* or *midwives to the Hebrews*, which may suggest that they were Egyptian. Lapsley points out that, if the midwives were indeed Egyptian, the theme of crossing ethnic boundaries (which forms a key theme in this text) would be even stronger, *Whispering the Word*, 72.

17. Lapsley, *Whispering the Word*, 80. See also Nancy Lee's intriguing argument that, in the rest of Exodus, even God does not comply with the work of the midwives, who save babies—perhaps even across ethnic boundaries. In sharp contrast to Pharaoh's daughter, whose decision to save a Hebrew baby was based on compassion (Lee argues), God did not secure the safety of either Egyptian or Hebrew children but killed the Egyptian firstborn in the same manner that Pharaoh abused his power, "Genocide's Lament: Moses, Pharaoh's Daughter, and the Former Yugoslavia," in *God in the Fray: A Tribute to Walter Brueggemann* (ed. Tod Linafelt and Timothy K. Beal; Minneapolis, MN: Fortress Press, 1998), 76–77.

18. Lapsley, *Whispering the Word*, 85; see also Lee, "Genocide's Lament," 74–75.

19. See Lapsley's argument that the midwives' speech can be read on two levels: the assertion that the women are like animals plays on Pharaoh's stereotyping of the Hebrews as less than human; on the other hand, it affirms that the Hebrews are able to thrive under difficult circumstances, *Whispering the Word*, 71.

20. Lee, "Genocide's Lament," 81. See also J. Cheryl Exum, "'You Shall Let Every Daughter Live': A Study of Exodus 1.8–2.10," *Semeia* 28 (1983): 63–82 (60).

21. Exum, "'You Shall Let Every Daughter Live,'" 56–57.

22. Lapsley, *Whispering the Word*, 87.

23. See also *Biblical Antiquities* (Pseudo-Philo), in which local chiefs are said to have replaced the midwives. Eileen Schuller, "Women of the Exodus in the Biblical Retellings of the Second Temple Period," in *Gender and Difference in Ancient Israel* (ed. Peggy L. Day; Minneapolis, MN: Fortress Press, 1989), 182–85. See also Cheryl Exum's argument that the positive portrayal of the women in this text only serves male interests; i.e., women working together to save the male savior, Moses, in "Second Thoughts about Secondary Characters: Women in

Exodus 1:8–2:10," in *A Feminist Companion to the Bible: Exodus to Deuteronomy* (ed. Athalya Brenner; Sheffield: Sheffield Academic Press, 2000), 75–84.

24. Carole Fontaine, "Disabilities and Illness in the Bible: A Feminist Perspective," in *A Feminist Companion to the Hebrew Bible in the New Testament* (ed. Athalya Brenner; Sheffield: Sheffield Academic Press, 1996), 297–98.

25. Wainwright, *Women Healing/Healing Women*, 96.

26. Wainwright argues that healing in the Hebrew Bible is typically portrayed as the task of the God of Israel. In Deut. 32:39, God is the one who kills and restores to life, who wounds and who heals. The only legitimate agents of healing are prophets such as Elijah and Elisha, while female prophets (such as Huldah and Miriam) are excluded from this role, in *Women Healing/Healing Women*, 92–96.

27. According to tradition, these were the dying words of Jesus on the cross (Mark 15:34; Matt. 27:46).

28. Ellen F. Davis, "Exploding the Limits: Form and Function in Psalm 22," *JSOT* 53 (1992): 97.

29. Davis, "Exploding the Limits," 97, 99. See also Patrick D. Miller, *They Cried to the Lord: The Form and Theology of Biblical Prayer* (Minneapolis, MN: Fortress Press, 1994), 114.

30. Mikhail M. Bakhtin, *Problems of Dostoevsky's Poetics* (ed. and trans. Caryl Emerson; Theory and History of Literature 8; Minneapolis, MN: University of Minnesota Press, 1984), 195; "Discourse in the Novel," in *The Dialogic Imagination: Four Essays* (ed. Caryl Emerson and Michael Holquist, trans. Michael Holquist; Austin, TX: University of Texas Press, 1981), 342–43.

31. John S. Kselman "'Why Have You Abandoned Me?' A Rhetorical Study of Psalm 22," in *Art and Meaning: Rhetoric in Biblical Literature* (ed. David J. A. Clines et al.; *JSOT* Sup. 19; Sheffield: JSOT, 1982), 184, 194; See also Miller, *They Cried to the Lord*, 114–15.

32. The etymology of the root γη9ψ is uncertain. However, according to Peter C. Craigie most scholars support the meaning "drew from the womb," *Psalms 1–50* (WBC; Waco TX: Word Books, 1983), 196.

33. The danger of childbirth is evident from the high mortality rate among females in their childbearing years. Carol L. Meyers points out that, whereas the life expectancy of men in biblical times was around forty, that of women was closer to thirty years of age, "The Roots of Restriction: Women in Early Israel," *BA* 41 (1978): 95; *Discovering Eve: Ancient Israelite Women in Context* (New York, NY: Oxford University Press, 1988), 112–13.

34. Phyllis Trible, *God and the Rhetoric of Sexuality* (OBT; Philadelphia, PA: Fortress Press, 1978), 38.

35. Trible, *God and the Rhetoric of Sexuality*, 60. See also Kselman, "'Why Have You Abandoned Me?'" 176–77.

36. Wendy Farley, *Tragic Vision and Divine Compassion: A Contemporary Theodicy* (Louisville, KY: Westminster John Knox Press, 1990), 113.

37. Carroll Stuhlmueller, *Psalms 1 (1–71)* (OTM 21; Wilmington, DE: Michael Glazier, 1983), 316.

38. Stuhlmueller, *Psalms 1*, 317; Hans-Joachim Kraus, *Psalms 60–150: A Commentary* (trans. Hilton C. Oswald; Minneapolis, MN: Augsburg Press, 1989), 71.

39. Samuel Balentine argues that, in a response to the disintegration of the royal

ideal and a growing disillusionment with the cult, Yehud in the postexilic period found meaning in the development of "a torah piety" that is characterized by "obedience to and trust in the torah of the Lord," "Politics of Religion," 130–37. James L. Mays demonstrates how "Torah—Psalms" like Psalms 1, 19, and 119 have transformed the function of the psalms to teach believers the way of righteousness, "The Place of Torah-Psalms in the Psalter," in James L. Mays, *The Lord Reigns: A Theological Handbook to the Psalms* (Louisville, KY: Westminster John Knox Press, 1994), 118–35.

40. James L. Crenshaw, "Life's Deepest Apprehension: Psalm 71," in James L. Crenshaw, *The Psalms: An Introduction* (Grand Rapids, MI: Wm. B. Eerdmans Publishing Co., 2001), 151, 153.

41. In *Lexicon in Veteris Testament Libros,* Ludwig Köhler and Walter Baumgartner interpret the verb גזה "to cut off" with reference to the action of cutting the umbilical cord. An alternative reading would be עוזזי (following the Targum and 4QPsᵃ), which is translated as "my strength." However, Mitchel Dahood warns against this easy solution and maintains that the more difficult reading is to be preferred, *Psalms 51–100* (AB; Garden City, NY: Doubleday, 1968), 173. Against this interpretation, Marvin Tate argues that v. 6b should read, "From my mother's womb, you have been my sustainer," proposing a participle form of גוז, meaning "my bearer/sustainer" (see also Num. 11:31—"being carried by the wind"), *Psalms 51–100,* 209.

42. Crenshaw, "Life's Deepest Apprehension," 151.

43. Keshgegian, *Redeeming Memories,* 234.

44. Keshgegian, *Redeeming Memories,* 65.

45. Keshgegian notes that this conviction is often triumphal in tone, celebrating the fact that, despite the perpetrators' best efforts, the survivors continue to survive and even to thrive. With reference to genocide, the survivors' economical and social success in their new country is regarded as evidence that genocide has failed, *Redeeming Memories,* 64.

46. Crenshaw, "Life's Deepest Apprehension," 143, 152.

47. Arthur Waskow, "Why Exodus Is Not Enough," *Cross Currents* (1990 Winter): 525–26. This poem forms part of an alternative Seder for Peace that includes references to contemporary examples of deep political and social divisions. See Rabbi Arthur Waskow, "The Passover of Peace: A Seder for the Children of Abraham, Hagar, and Sarah," http://www.shalomctr.org/node/186. Accessed February 22, 2009.

48. In his essay, "Midwives of Democracy: The Role of Churches in Democratic Transition in South Africa," *JTSA* 86 (1994): 14, John de Gruchy cites a speech by former President Nelson Mandela who, in 1992, praised the Ethiopian church and the ecumenical movement for their key role in the struggle against apartheid. Mandela said, "The church in our country has no option but to join other agents of change and transformation in the difficult task of acting as midwife to the birth of our democracy and acting as one of the institutions that will nurture and entrench it in our society."

49. Sharon D. Welch, *Sweet Dreams in America: Making Ethics and Spirituality Work* (New York, NY: Routledge, 1999), 133.

50. Paul D. Hanson, "Divine Power in Powerlessness," in *Power, Powerlessness, and the Divine: New Inquiries in Bible and Theology* (ed. Cynthia L. Rigby; Atlanta, GA: Scholars Press, 1997), 198.

Chapter 5: God's Delivering Presence

1. Teresa Berger, "Fragments of a Vision in a September 11 World," in *Strike Terror No More: Theology, Ethics and the New War* (ed. Jon L. Berquist; St. Louis, MS: Chalice Press, 2002), 110–11.

2. David J. A. Clines, *I, He, We, They: A Literary Approach to Isaiah 53* (JSOT Sup.1; Sheffield: JSOT Press, 1976), 54.

3. Melissa Raphael, *The Female Face of God in Auschwitz: A Jewish Feminist Theology of the Holocaust* (Religion and Gender; London: Routledge, 2003).

4. As Megillah 29a states, "Come and see how beloved Israel is before God; for whenever they went into exile the Shekhinah went with them. When they were exiled to Egypt, the Shekhinah went with them, in Babylon the Shekhinah was with them, and in the future, when Israel will be redeemed, the Shekhinah will be with them." This image of a "homeless" God resonates with the words of one of Andrea Fröchtling's interviewees from South Africa, "When we were forced removed, they destroyed our church as well, so God, he no longer had a home, God was homeless, and we also, we were homeless. So God, he couldn't stay in Doornkop, he must go with us into exile. And that he did. And when we came back, God, he came back with us," Andrea Fröchtling, *Exiled God and Exiled Peoples: Passionis and the Perception of God during and after Apartheid and Shoah* (Ökumenische Studien 22; Berlin-Hamburg-Münster: LIT Verlag, 2002), 243.

5. Raphael, *Female Face of God*, 82, 128.

6. Flora Keshgegian, *Time for Hope: Practices for Living in Today's World* (New York, NY: Continuum, 2006), 131–32.

7. bell hooks, *Teaching Community: A Pedagogy of Hope* (London: Routledge, 2003), xiv.

8. Raphael, *Female Face of God*, 36.

9. See, e.g., Eliezer Berkovits, *Faith after the Holocaust* (New York, NY: KTAV, 1973); Martin Buber, *The Eclipse of God: Studies in the Relation between Religion and Philosophy* (London: Gollancz, 1953); Emmanuel Levinas, "Loving the Torah More than God," in Zvi Kolitz, *Yosl Rakover Talks to God* (trans. Carol Brown Janeway; New York, NY: Pantheon Books, 1999).

10. Raphael, *Female Face of God*, 47.

11. David R. Blumenthal, *Facing the Abusing God: A Theology of Protest* (Louisville, KY: Westminster John Knox Press, 1993), 205. See also Raphael's discussion of Blumenthal's work in *Female Face of God*, 47–50.

12. Elie Wiesel, *The Accident* (New York, NY: Hill and Wang, 1997), 92.

13. Raphael, *Female Face of God*, 88.

14. Raphael, *Female Face of God*, 96–97, 112.

15. Raphael, *Female Face of God*, 60–61.

16. Olga Lengyel, *Five Chimneys* (New York, NY: Howard Fertig Publisher, 1995), 123. Cited in Raphael, *Female Face of God*, 69.

17. Raphael, *Female Face of God*, 81.

18. Raphael, *Female Face of God*, 51.

19. Raphael, *Female Face of God*, 58.

20. Raphael, *Female Face of God*, 115. See also Elizabeth A. Johnson, who argues that "[God] the Holy One is powerfully near in and through the wondrous processes of nature, the history of struggle for freedom and life, and communities where justice and peace prevail." *Friends of God and Prophets: A*

Feminist Theological Reading of the Communion of Saints (Sheffield: Continuum, 1999), 55.

21. Raphael, *Female Face of God*, 152. See Janet Martin Soskice's book, *The Kindness of God: Metaphor, Gender and Religious Language,* in which she argues that, in Middle English, the words "kind" and "kin" were the same, suggesting to her that kindness and kinship are intrinsically related (Oxford: Oxford University Press, 2007), 5–6.

22. Raphael, *Female Face of God*, 44.

23. Keshgegian, *Time for Hope*, 166.

24. Flora Keshgegian, *Redeeming Memories: A Theology of Healing and Transformation* (Nashville, TN: Abingdon Press, 2000), 235.

25. Keshgegian, *Time for Hope*, 86.

26. Raphael, *Female Face of God*, 57. Such an understanding of our own role in God's liberation or redemption challenges us to embrace the open-endedness of the present and future; realizing that, as Keshgegian proposes, even though "we cannot control the play," we may participate in this wonderfully complex and intricate drama called life, *Time for Hope*, 159, 166.

27. Sharon Welch, *A Feminist Ethic of Risk* (Minneapolis, MN: Fortress Press, 1990), 180.

28. Welch, *Feminist Ethic of Risk*, 173, 178.

29. Raphael, *Female Face of God*, 115. See Elizabeth A. Johnson's well-known saying: "The symbol of God functions." The language and images we use for God have the power to shape people's perceptions, behavior, and actions, *She Who Is: The Mystery of God in Feminist Theological Discourse* (New York, NY: Crossroad, 1992), 4.

30. Raphael writes that "in the (very dim) light of Auschwitz, such a God might be dismissed as a mere shadow passing over, a passive, useless God whose lack of the traditional attribute of omnipotence abandons Jewry to its fate, now even more frighteningly vulnerable to harm than it was before. But a maternal God leaves Israel no more vulnerable than was empirically the case under a theology of divine omnipotence for which there was, in any case, little or no evidence," *Female Face of God*, 127.

31. Johnson, *She Who Is*, 266–67. See also Raphael, *Female Face of God*, 41.

32. Raphael, *Female Face of God*, 90–91.

33. Raphael, *Female Face of God*, 94.

34. Raphael refers to the example of Janusz Korczak's care for the orphans in his children's home in the Warsaw ghetto, whose acts of "mothering" these orphans until their death in Treblinka are, according to Raphael, "but one demonstration that care is a function of all Israel—men and women—as itself a sanctified familial community," *Female Face of God*, 10.

35. Johnson, *Friends of God and Prophets*, 141.

36. Rachel Naomi Remen, "Educating for Mission, Meaning, and Compassion," in *The Heart of Learning: Spirituality in Education* (ed. Steven Glazer; New York, NY: Jeremy P. Tarcher, 1999), 33–49 (35). With reference to Remen's challenge, bell hooks argues that, "This is the vision of transformative education. It is education as the practice of freedom," *Teaching Community*, 181.

37. hooks, *Teaching Community*, xiv. See Paulo Freire, *A Pedagogy of Hope: Reliving Pedagogy of the Oppressed* (London: Continuum, 1995).

38. Johnson identifies four practices of memory that are important in a feminist theological approach to biblical and Christian tradition. In her book she seeks to (1) recover lost memory [Hagar]; (2) rectify the distorted story [Mary Magdalene]; (3) reassess value [the Virgin Martyrs]; (4) reclaim the silence [the myriad of anonymous women], *Friends of God and Prophets*, 141–62.

39. Johnson, *Friends of God and Prophets*, 145–46.

40. Johnson, *Friends of God and Prophets*, 161.

41. Keshgegian, *Redeeming Memories*, 145. See also Johnson, *Friends of God and Prophets*, 155–56.

42. Keshgegian, *Redeeming Memories*, 131.

43. hooks, *Teaching Community*, xix. Parker Palmer says, "Here the act of knowing is an act of love, the act of entertaining and embracing the reality of the other, of allowing the other to enter and embrace our own. In such knowing we know and are known as members of one community," *To Know as We Are Known: A Spirituality of Education* (San Francisco, CA; Harper and Row, 1983), 8.

44. Rita Nakashima Brock, *Journeys of the Heart: A Christology of Erotic Power* (New York, NY: Crossroad, 1991), 47–48.

45. Rachel Naomi Remen, "Educating for Mission, Meaning, and Compassion," in *The Heart of Learning: Spirituality in Education* (ed. Steven Glazer; New York, NY: Jeremy P. Tarcher, 1999), 34.

46. Johnson argues that by "reconceptualizing the whole" we are making "room for women to exist as subjects of history, now as then," *Friends of God and Prophets*, 161.

47. South Africa has one of the highest statistics of rape and abuse in the world. In a recent study undertaken by the Medical Research Council in the Eastern Cape, it was found that 27.6 percent of 1,738 men interviewed admitted to having raped a woman. For the news story, see "South Africa: One in Four Men Rape," IRINNews, June 18, 2009. http://www.irinnews.org/Report.aspx ?ReportId=84909. Accessed August 9, 2009. According to statistics on the Rape, Abuse, and Incest National Network, this reality is a global phenomenon (www.rainn.org).

48. In this regard, Flora Keshgegian spends the last chapter of her book *Redeeming Memories* on "The Church as a Community of Remembrance and Witness," in which she outlines the significance of faith communities coming together to remember authentically. For instance, Keshgegian says that where believers gather in worship services to "remember and to re-member itself in relation to God," there are various elements that can be fruitfully employed for communities to deal with their grief, 218–26.

49. See Kathleen D. Billman and Daniel L. Migliore's plea for recovering lament in the worship of the church in their book *Rachel's Cry: Prayer of Lament and Rebirth of Hope* (Cleveland, OH: United Church Press, 1999), 19.

50. Denise Ackermann, "Lamenting Tragedy from 'The Other Side,'" in *Sameness and Difference: Problems and Potentials in South African Civil Society* (ed. James R. Cochrane and Bastienne Klein; South Africa Philosophical Studies 1; Washington, DC: Council for Research in Values and Philosophy, 2000), 232.

51. In light of the collective guilt of the white population ("my people"), who largely have been oblivious either to their active (or inert) role in apartheid or at the very least to the ways in which they have benefited at the cost of the

other, Ackermann proposes that public acts of lament should be preceded by "public acts of repentance," maintaining that this "public lament for the injustice and the torments of the past is a potentially healing way of responding to the past," "Lamenting Tragedy from 'The Other Side,'" 231.

52. Litany by Ann Heidkamp, from *No Longer Strangers: A Resource for Women and Worship* by Iben Gjerding and Katherine Kinnamon. World Council of Churches Publication, 1983. Adapted by Rev. Margaret Rose for the Opening Liturgy for the Anglican Delegation to the UN/CSW; February 27, 2004; Chapel of Christ the Lord, Episcopal Church Center, New York City. Quoted in Johnson, *Friends of God and Prophets*, 256.

53. Raphael, *Female Face of God*, 31.

54. Hymn 2048, "God Weeps," words: Shirley Erena Murray, music: Carlton R. Young, in *The Faith We Sing* (Nashville, TN: Abingdon Press, 2000).

55. Hymn 2050, "Mothering God, You Gave Us Birth," words: Jean Janzen, based on the writings of Julian of Norwich, music: H. Percy Smith, in *The Faith We Sing* (Nashville, TN: Abingdon Press, 2000).

56. Hymn 2047, "Bring Many Names," words: Brian Wren, music: Carlton R. Young, in *The Faith We Sing,* (Nashville, TN: Abingdon Press, 2000).

57. Walter Brueggemann, comment made during a Society of Biblical Literature session on "God and Metaphor in the Prophets," San Antonio, TX, 2004.

Bibliography

Ackerman, Susan. *Warrior, Dancer, Seductress, Queen: Women in Judges and Biblical Israel*. Anchor Bible Reference Library. New York, NY: Doubleday, 2002.

Ackermann, Denise M. "Lamenting Tragedy from 'The Other Side.'" In *Sameness and Difference: Problems and Potentials in South African Civil Society*. Edited by James R. Cochrane and Bastienne Klein, 313–42. South Africa Philosophical Studies 1. Washington, DC: Council for Research in Values and Philosophy, 2000.

——. "On Hearing and Lamenting: Faith and Truth Telling." In *To Remember and to Heal: Theological and Psychological Reflections on Truth and Reconciliation*. Edited by H. Russel Botman and Robin M. Petersen, 47–56. Cape Town: Human and Rousseau Uitgewers, 1996.

Albertz, Rainer. *Israel in Exile: The History and Literature of the Sixth Century BCE*. Translated by David Green. Atlanta, GA: Society of Biblical Literature, 2003.

Ateek, Naim Stifan. "A Palestine Perspective: The Bible and Liberation." In *Voices from the Margin: Interpreting the Bible in the Third World*. Edited by R. S. Sugirtharajah, 280–86. Maryknoll, NY: Orbis Books, 1991.

Baker-Fletcher, Karen. *Dancing with God: The Trinity from a Womanist Perspective*. St. Louis, MS: Chalice Press, 2007.

Bakhtin, Mikhail M. "Discourse in the Novel." In *The Dialogic Imagination: Four Essays*. Edited by Caryl Emerson and Michael Holquist, 259–422. Translated by Michael Holquist. Austin, TX: University of Texas Press, 1981.

——. *Problems of Dostoevsky's Poetics*. Edited and translated by Caryl Emerson. Theory and History of Literature 8. Minneapolis, MN: University of Minnesota Press, 1984.

Balentine, Samuel E. "The Politics of Religion in the Persian Period." In *After the Exile: Essays in Honour of Rex Mason*. Edited by John Barton and David J. Reimer, 129–46. Macon, GA: Mercer University Press, 1996.

Basser, Herbert W. "A Love for All Seasons: Weeping in Jewish Sources." In *Holy Tears:*

Weeping in the Religious Imagination. Edited by Kimberley Christine Patton and John Stratton Hawley, 178–200. Princeton, NJ: Princeton University Press, 2005.

Berger, Teresa. "Fragments of a Vision in a September 11 World." In *Strike Terror No More: Theology, Ethics and the New War.* Edited by Jon L. Berquist, 110–11. St. Louis, MS: Chalice Press, 2002.

Beuken, Willem A. M. "The Main Theme of Trito-Isaiah 'The Servants of YHWH.'" *Journal for the Study of the Old Testament* 47 (1990): 67–87.

Billman, Kathleen D. and Daniel L. Migliore. *Rachel's Cry: Prayer of Lament and Rebirth of Hope.* Cleveland, OH: United Church Press, 1999.

Bleeker, Claas Jouco. "Isis and Nephthys as Wailing Women." *Numen* 5 (1958): 1–17.

Blenkinsopp, Joseph. "Second Isaiah—Prophet of Universalism." *Journal for the Study of the Old Testament* 41 (1988): 83–103.

Blumenthal, David R. *Facing the Abusing God: A Theology of Protest.* Louisville, KY: Westminster John Knox, 1993.

Braiterman, Zachary. *(God) after Auschwitz: Tradition and Change in Post-Holocaust Jewish Thought.* Princeton, NJ: Princeton University Press, 1998.

Brenner, Athalya. *The Israelite Woman: Social Role and Literary Type in Biblical Narrative.* Sheffield: JSOT, 1985.

Brock, Rita Nakashima. *Journeys of the Heart: A Christology of Erotic Power.* New York, NY: Crossroad, 1991.

———. "A New Thing in the Land: The Female Surrounds the Warrior." In *Power, Powerlessness, and the Divine: New Inquiries in Bible and Theology.* Edited by Cynthia L. Rigby, 137–59. Atlanta, GA: Scholars Press, 1997.

Bronner, Leila Leah. "Gynomorphic Imagery in Exilic Isaiah 40–66." *Dor le Dor* 12 (1983–84): 71–83.

Brueggemann, Walter. "Alien Witness: How God's People Challenge Empire." *Christian Century* (March 6, 2007): 28–32.

———. "Faith at the *Nullpunkt.*" In *The End of the World and the Ends of God: Science and Theology on Eschatology.* Edited by John Polkinghorne and Michael Welker, 143–54. Harrisburg, PA.: Trinity, 2000.

———. *Isaiah 40–66.* Westminster Bible Companion; Louisville, KY: Westminster John Knox Press, 1998.

———. *To Pluck Up, to Tear Down: A Commentary on the Book of Jeremiah 1–25.* International Theological Commentary. Grand Rapids, MI: Wm. B. Eerdmans Publishing Co., 1988.

Buber, Martin. *The Eclipse of God: Studies in the Relation between Religion and Philosophy.* London: Gollancz, 1953.

Carroll, Robert P. "The Myth of the Empty Land." *Semeia* 59 (1992): 79–93.

Chirongoma, Sophia. "Women, Poverty, and HIV in Zimbabwe: An Exploration of Inequalities in Health Care." In *Africa Women, Religion, and Health: Essays in Honor of Mercy Amba Ewudziwa Oduyoye.* Edited by Isabel Phiri and Sarojini Nadar, 173–86. Pietermaritzburg: Cluster Publications, 2000.

Cilliers, Johan. *God for Us? An Analysis and Assessment of Dutch Reformed Preaching during the Apartheid Years.* Stellenbosch: Sun Press, 2006.

Clines, David J. A. *I, He, We, They: A Literary Approach to Isaiah 53. Journal for the Study of the Old Testament* Sup.1 (1976).

Crenshaw, James L. "Life's Deepest Apprehension: Psalm 71." In *The Psalms: An Introduction,* 142–54. Grand Rapids, MI: Wm. B. Eerdmans Publishing Co., 2001.

Dahood, Mitchel. *Psalms 51–100.* Anchor Bible. Garden City, NY: Doubleday, 1968.

Darr, Katheryn Pfisterer. "Like Warrior, like Woman: Destruction and Deliverance in Isaiah 42:10–17." *Catholic Biblical Quarterly* 49 (1987): 564–65.

———. "Two Unifying Female Images in the Book of Isaiah." In *Uncovering Ancient Stones: Essays in Memory of H. Niel Richardson*. Edited by Lewis M. Hopfe, 17–30. Winona Lake, ID: Eisenbrauns, 1994.

Davis, Ellen F. "Exploding the Limits: Form and Function in Psalm 22." *Journal for the Study of the Old Testament* 53 (1992): 93–105.

de Gruchy, John. "Midwives of Democracy: The Role of Churches in Democratic Transition in South Africa." *Journal of Theology for Southern Africa* 86 (1994): 14–25.

Deist, Ferdinand. "The Dangers of Deuteronomy: A Page from the Reception History of the Book." In *Studies in Deuteronomy: In Honour of C. J. Labuschagne on the Occasion of His 65th Birthday*. Edited by Florentino García Martínez, 13–29. Leiden: E. J. Brill, 1994.

Dille, Sarah J. *Mixing Metaphors: God as Mother and Father in Deutero-Isaiah*. Journal for the Study of the Old Testament Supplement, 398. Gender, Culture, Theory Series, 13. London: T & T Clark International, 2004.

Dube, Musa. "Jumping the Fire with Judith: Postcolonial Feminist Hermeneutics of Liberation." In *Feminist Interpretation of the Bible and the Hermeneutics of Liberation*. Edited by Silvia Schroer and Sophia Bietenhard, 60–76. London: Sheffield Academic Press, 2003.

Ehrenreich, Barbara and Deirdre English. *Witches, Midwives, and Nurses: A History of Women Healers*. New York, NY: Feminist Press, 1973.

Exum, J. Cheryl. "'You Shall Let Every Daughter Live': A Study of Exodus 1.8–2.10." *Semeia* 28 (1983): 63–82.

Farley, Wendy. *Tragic Vision and Divine Compassion: A Contemporary Theodicy*. Louisville, KY: Westminster John Knox, 1990.

Felman, Shoshana. "Education and Crisis." In *Trauma: Explorations in Memory*. Edited by Cathy Caruth, 13–60. Baltimore, MD: John Hopkins University Press, 1995.

Fontaine, Carole. "Disabilities and Illness in the Bible: A Feminist Perspective." *A Feminist Companion to the Hebrew Bible in the New Testament*. Edited by Athalya Brenner, 286–300. Sheffield: Sheffield Academic Press, 1996.

Freire, Paulo. *A Pedagogy of Hope: Reliving Pedagogy of the Oppressed*. London: Continuum, 1995.

Fretheim, Terence E. *Jeremiah*. Smyth and Helwys Bible Commentary. Macon, GA: Smyth and Helwys, 2002.

———. *The Suffering of God*. Overtures to Biblical Theology. Minneapolis, MN: Fortress Press, 1984.

Fröchtling, Andrea. *Exiled God and Exiled Peoples: Memoria Passionis and the Perception of God during and after Apartheid and Shoah*. Ökumenische Studien 22. Berlin-Hamburg-Münster: LIT Verlag, 2002.

Gamliel, Tova "Performance Versus Social Invisibility: What Can Be Learned from the Wailing Culture of Old-Age Yemenite-Jewish Women?" *Women Studies International Forum*, 31/3(May–June 2008): 209–218.

———. "'Wailing Lore' in a Yemenite–Israeli Community: Bereavement, Expertise, and Therapy." *Social Science and Medicine*, 65/7(2007): 1501–1511.

Garber, David G. "Facing Traumatizing Texts: Reading Nahum's Nationalistic Rage," *Review and Expositor*, 105/2 (2008): 285–94.

Gibbs, Robert. *Why Ethics? Signs of Responsibility*. Princeton, NJ: Princeton University Press, 2000.

Gobodo-Madikizela, Pumla. *A Human Being Died That Night: A South African Woman Confronts the Legacy of Apartheid*. Boston, MA: Houghton Mifflin Co., 2003.

Goitein, S. D. "Women as Creators of Biblical Genres," *Prooftexts* 8/1 (1988): 1–33.

Gruber, Mayer I. "The Motherhood of God in Second Isaiah." *Revue Biblique* 90 (1983): 351–59.

Hanson, Paul D. "Divine Power in Powerlessness." In *Power, Powerlessness, and the Divine: New Inquiries in Bible and Theology*. Edited by Cynthia L. Rigby, 179–97; Atlanta, GA: Scholars Press, 1997.

———. *Isaiah 40–66*. Interpretation. Louisville, KY: Westminster John Knox, 1995.

———. *The People Called: The Growth of Community in the Bible*. San Francisco, CA: Harper and Row, 1987.

Hens-Piazza, Gina. *Nameless, Blameless, and Without Shame: Two Cannibal Mothers before a King*. Collegeville, MN: Liturgical Press, 2003.

hooks, bell. *Teaching Community: A Pedagogy of Hope*. London: Routledge, 2003.

Ilan, Tal. *Jewish Women in Greco-Roman Palestine*. Peabody, MA: Hendrickson, 1996.

Johnson, Elizabeth A. *Friends of God and Prophets: A Feminist Theological Reading of the Communion of Saints*. Sheffield: Continuum, 1999.

———. *She Who Is: The Mystery of God in Feminist Theological Discourse*. New York, NY: Crossroad, 1992.

Johnston, Ann. "A Prophetic Vision of an Alternative Community: A Reading of Isaiah 40–55." In *Uncovering Ancient Stones: Essays in Memory of H. Neil Richardson*. Edited by Lewis M. Hopfe, 31–40. Winona Lake, ID: Eisenbrauns, 1994.

Kaminsky, Joel. *Yet I Loved Jacob: Reclaiming the Biblical Concept of Election*. Nashville, TN: Abingdon Press, 2007.

Keller, Catherine. "The Armageddon of 9/11: Lament for the New Millennium." In *God and Power: Counter-Apocalyptic Journeys*, 3–16. Minneapolis, MN: Fortress Press, 2005.

———. "The Love of Postcolonialism: Theology in the Interstices of Empire." In *Postcolonial Theologies: Divinity and Empire*. Edited by Catherine Keller et al., 221–42. St. Louis, MS: Chalice Press, 2004.

———. "The Love Supplement: Christianity and Empire." In *God and Power: Counter-Apocalyptic Journeys*, 113–34. Minneapolis, MN: Fortress Press, 2005.

———. "Ms.Calculating the Endtimes: Gender Styles of Apocalypse." *God and Power: Counter-Apocalyptic Journeys*, 53–66. Minneapolis, MN: Fortress Press, 2005.

———. "Preemption and Omnipotence: A Niebuhrian Prophecy." In *God and Power: Counter-Apocalyptic Journeys*, 17–34. Minneapolis, MN: Fortress Press, 2005.

Keshgegian, Flora A. *Redeeming Memories: A Theology of Healing and Transformation*. Nashville, TN: Abingdon Press, 2000.

———. *Time for Hope: Practices for Living in Today's World*. New York, NY: Continuum, 2006.

Kraus, Hans-Joachim. *Psalms 60–150: A Commentary*. Translated by Hilton C. Oswald. Minneapolis, MN: Augsburg Press, 1989.

Kselman, John S. "'Why Have You Abandoned Me?' A Rhetorical Study of Psalm 22." In *Art and Meaning: Rhetoric in Biblical Literature*. Edited by David J. A. Clines et al., 172–98. Journal for the Study of the Old Testament Supplement, 19. Sheffield: JSOT, 1982.

Lapsley, Jacqueline E. *Whispering the Word: Hearing Women's Stories in the Old Testament*. Louisville, KY: Westminster John Knox Press, 2005.

Lee, Nancy. "Genocide's Lament: Moses, Pharaoh's Daughter, and the Former Yugoslavia." In *God in the Fray: A Tribute to Walter Brueggemann*. Edited by Tod Linafelt and Timothy K. Beal, 66–82. Minneapolis, MN: Fortress Press, 1998.

Levinas, Emmanuel. "Loving the Torah More than God." In Zvi Kolitz, *Yosl Rakover Talks to God*. Translated by Carol Brown Janeway, 79–87. New York, NY: Pantheon Books, 1999.

Levine, Herbert J. *Sing unto God a New Song: A Contemporary Reading of the Psalms*. Bloomington, IN: Indiana University Press, 1995.

Lundbom, Jack R. *Jeremiah 1–20*. Anchor Bible 21A. New York, NY: Doubleday, 1999.

Lutz, Tom *Crying: The Natural and Cultural History of Tears*. New York, NY: W. W. Norton and Co., 1999.

Mays, James L. "The Place of Torah-Psalms in the Psalter." In *The Lord Reigns: A Theological Handbook to the Psalms*. Louisville, KY: Westminster John Knox Press, 1994.

———. *Psalms*. Interpretation. Louisville, KY: John Knox Press, 1994.

Meyers, Carol L. *Discovering Eve: Ancient Israelite Women in Context*. New York, NY: Oxford University Press, 1988.

———"The Roots of Restriction: Women in Early Israel." *Biblical Archaeologist* 41(1978): 91–103.

Miller, Patrick D. *They Cried to the Lord: The Form and Theology of Biblical Prayer*. Minneapolis, MN: Fortress Press, 1994.

Muilenburg, James. "The Book of Isaiah." In *The Interpreter's Bible*, Vol. 5. Nashville, TN: Abingdon Press, 1956.

Niditch, Susan. "Eroticism and Death in the Tale of Jael." In *Women in the Hebrew Bible*. Edited by Alice Bach, 305–76. New York, NY: Routledge, 1999.

O'Brien, Julia. *Challenging Prophetic Metaphor: Theology and Ideology in the Prophets*. Louisville, KY: Westminster John Knox Press, 2008.

O'Connor, Kathleen M. "A Family Comes Undone." *Review and Expositor* 105/2 (2008): 201–12.

———. "Rekindling Life, Igniting Hope," *Journal for Preachers* 30/2 (Lent 2007): 30–34.

———. "The Tears of God and Divine Character in Jeremiah 2–9." In *God in the Fray: A Tribute to Walter Brueggemann*. Edited by Tod Linafelt and Timothy K. Beal, 172–85. Minneapolis, MN: Fortress Press, 1998.

Patton, K. C. and Hawley, J. S. eds. *Holy Tears: Weeping in the Religious Imagination*. Princeton, NJ: Princeton University Press, 2005.

Raphael, Melissa. *The Female Face of God in Auschwitz: A Jewish Feminist Theology of the Holocaust*. Religion and Gender. London: Routledge, 2003.

Remen, Rachel Naomi. "Educating for Mission, Meaning, and Compassion." In *The Heart of Learning: Spirituality in Education*. Edited by Steven Glazer, 33–49. New York, NY: Jeremy P. Tarcher, 1999.

Rubenstein, Richard. *After Auschwitz: Radical Theology and Contemporary Judaism*. Indianapolis, IN: Bobbs-Merrill, 1966.

Ruddick, Sara. *Maternal Thinking: Toward a Politics of Peace*. New York, NY: Ballantine Books, 1989.

Said, Edward. "Reflections on Exile." In *Reflections on Exile and Other Essays*. Cambridge, MA: Harvard University Press, 2000.

Sands, Kathleen. "Tragedy, Theology, and Feminism in the Time aftr Time," *New Literary History* 35/1 (2004): 43.

Sawyer, Deborah. *God, Gender, and the Bible*. New York, NY: Routledge, 2002.

Scalise, Pamela J. "The Way of Weeping: Reading the Path of Grief in Jeremiah," *Word and World* 22/4 (2002): 415–22.

Schmitt, John J. "The Motherhood of God and Zion as Mother." *Revue Biblique* 92 (1985): 557–69.

Schuller, Eileen. "Women of the Exodus in the Biblical Retellings of the Second Temple Period." In *Gender and Difference in Ancient Israel*. Edited by Peggy L. Day, 178–94. Minneapolis, MN: Fortress, 1989.

Schüssler Fiorenza, Elisabeth. *The Power of the Word: Scripture and the Rhetoric of Empire.* Minneapolis, MN: Fortress Press, 2007.

Scott, James C. *Domination and the Art of Resistance: Hidden Transcripts.* New Haven, CT: Yale University Press, 1992.

Smith-Christopher, Daniel L. *A Biblical Theology of Exile.* Overtures to Biblical Theology. Minneapolis, MN: Fortress Press, 2001.

Song, Chuan-Seng. *The Tears of Lady Meng: A Parable of People's Political Theology.* Maryknoll, NY: Orbis Books, 1981.

Soskice, Janet Martin. *The Kindness of God: Metaphor, Gender, and Religious Language.* Oxford: Oxford University Press, 2007.

Spivak, Gayatri Chakravorty. "Can the Subaltern Speak?" In *Marxism and the Interpretation of Culture.* Edited by Cary Nelson and Lawrence Grossberg. London: Macmillan, 1988.

————. *A Critique of Postcolonial Reason: Toward a History of the Vanishing Present.* Cambridge, MA: Harvard University Press, 1999.

Stuhlmueller, Carroll. *Psalms 1 (1–71).* Old Testament Message 21. Wilmington, DE: Michael Glazier, 1983.

Stulman, Louis. *Order amid Chaos: Jeremiah as Symbolic Tapestry.* Sheffield: Sheffield Academic Press, 1998.

Sweeney, Marvin. *Reading the Hebrew Bible after the Shoah.* Minneapolis, MN: Fortress Press, 2008.

Tate, Marvin E. *Psalms 51–100.* Word Biblical Commentary. Dallas, TX: Word Books, 1990.

Trible, Phyllis. *God and the Rhetoric of Sexuality.* Overtures to Biblical Theology. Philadelphia, PA: Fortress Press, 1978.

van Dijk-Hemmes, Fokkelien. "Traces of Women's Texts in the Hebrew Bible." In *On Gendering Texts: Female and Male Voices in the Hebrew Bible.* Edited by Athalya Brenner and Fokkelien van Dijk-Hemmes, 71–83. Biblical Interpretation Series 1. Leiden: Brill, 1993.

Wainwright, Elaine. *Women Healing/Healing Women: The Genderization of Healing in Early Christianity.* London: Equinox Publishing, 2006.

Warrior, Robert Allen. "A Native American Perspective: Canaanite, Cowboys, and Indians." In *Voices from the Margin: Interpreting the Bible in the Third World.* Edited by R. S. Sugirtharajah, 287–95. Maryknoll, NY: Orbis Books, 1991.

Waskow, Arthur. "Why Exodus Is Not Enough," *Cross Currents* (1990 Winter): 525–26.

Weems, Renita. *Battered Love: Marriage, Sex, and Violence in the Hebrew Prophets.* Overtures to Biblical Theology. Minneapolis, MN: Fortress Press, 1995.

Welch, Sharon D. *A Feminist Ethic of Risk.* Minneapolis, MN: Fortress Press, 1990.

————. *Sweet Dreams in America: Making Ethics and Spirituality Work.* New York, NY: Routledge, 1999.

Willey, Patricia Tull. *Remember the Former Things: The Recollection of Previous Texts in Second Isaiah.* Atlanta, GA: Scholars Press, 1997.

Wolterstorff, Nicholas. *Lament for a Son.* Grand Rapids, MI: Wm. B. Eerdmans Publishing Co., 1987.

————. "The Wounds of God: Calvin's Theology of Social Justice." *The Reformed Journal* 37/6 (1987): 14–22.

Yee, Gale. "By the Hand of a Woman: The Metaphor of the Woman Warrior in Judges 4." *Semeia* 61 (1993): 116–25.

————. *Poor Banished Children of Eve: Woman as Evil in the Hebrew Bible.* Minneapolis, MN: Augsburg Fortress Press, 2003.

Permissions

"Rupturing God-language: The Metaphor of God as Midwife in Psalm 22," by L. Juliana Claassens, from *Engaging the Bible in a Gendered World: An Introduction to Feminist Biblical Interpretation in Honor of Katharine Doob Sakenfeld*, edited by Linda Day and Carolyn Pressler (Louisville, KY: Westminster John Knox Press, 2006). Reprinted by permission of Westminster John Knox Press. All rights reserved.

"Weeping," composed by Dan Heymann and published by Muffled Music (administered by Kobalt Music/Sheer Music) and Geoff Paynter Music Publishing, is reproduced with permision. All rights reserved. For more on this song cf. http://www.weeping.info/index.html.

"Why Exodus Is Not Enough," by Arthur Waskow, from *Cross Currents* (Winter 1990), is reproduced with permission. All rights reserved.

CPSIA information can be obtained
at www.ICGtesting.com
Printed in the USA
LVOW12s2002110416
483088LV00031B/1747/P